Block Scheduling Handbook
with Team Teaching Strategies

HOLT
CALL TO FREEDOM

Beginnings to 1877

D1512591

HOLT, RINEHART AND WINSTON
A Harcourt Education Company

Austin · New York · Orlando · Atlanta · San Francisco · Boston · Dallas · Toronto · London

Cover: Christie's Images

Printed in the United States of America

ISBN 0-03-065224-3

1 2 3 4 5 6 7 8 9   085   04 03 02 01

★ BLOCK SCHEDULING HANDBOOK ★

★ TO THE TEACHER ★

Block Scheduling Handbook
with Team Teaching Strategies

Each chapter of *Call to Freedom: Beginnings to 1877* has a corresponding lesson plan to meet the needs of block scheduling programs. These lesson plans provide motivational activities, a wide range of teaching strategies geared toward different learning styles and levels, and suggestions for lessons extensions, review, assessment, and reteaching in a block scheduling environment.

Additionally, each chapter has a Team Teaching Strategy that enables historical subjects to be examined through other disciplines. For the most part these strategies focus on links between history and literature, thus providing students with the opportunity to gain new insight into events of the past. Students will also be able to work on projects that demonstrate their understanding of both disciplines and that provide a method of alternative assessment.

★ ★

BLOCK SCHEDULING LESSON PLANS

THINK ABOUT THEMES

Culture

Agree The environment creates situations that culture groups within it must respond to.

Disagree Many aspects of a culture group, such as marriage ceremonies, are independent of the environment.

Geography

Agree A group cannot survive if it is unable to grow what it needs to eat.

Disagree A group's survival is dependent upon its knowledge.

Global Relations

Agree Nations that do not trade with other countries cannot survive.

Disagree A nation's strength is determined by its own resources.

LESSON 1

(For use with Sections 1 and 2, pp. 4–16)

OBJECTIVES

1. Explain how the first people arrived in America and why the development of agriculture was important to them.

2. Identify the significant aspects, accomplishments, and societies of early Mesoamerican and North American cultures.

3. Explain how the environment influenced Native American cultures.

4. Examine the various traits of Native Americans, including types of housing, in different culture areas.

LET'S GET STARTED!

Write the following terms on the chalkboard: *art, customs, language, religious beliefs, sense of identity.* Explain to students that these are all characteristics that make up a people's culture. Have small groups of students list different aspects and examples of these characteristics. Tell students that in this lesson, they will learn about the development of cultures in North America and Mesoamerica.

TEACH OBJECTIVE 1

All Levels: Using the graphic organizer on page 6, lead a class discussion about why the development of agriculture was important to early American societies. Then organize students into small groups. Have each group create a "What If?" scenario about what life would have been like if these societies had never developed agriculture. **[English Language Learners, Cooperative Learning]**

Level 3: Organize students into small groups. Tell groups to imagine that they are Paleo-Indians who have recently arrived in the Americas. Have groups create a documentary about their journey to North America. **[Cooperative Learning]**

TEACH OBJECTIVE 2

All Levels: Have volunteers tell you the names of the early Mesoamerican and North American cultures they have studied in the chapter. Write these names down on slips of paper and put the slips in a hat. Then organize the class into small groups and provide each group with a piece of butcher paper and colored pencils. Have each group choose a slip of paper. Direct each group to create a scene that illustrates the significant aspects and accomplishments of their culture group. **[English Language Learners, Cooperative Learning]**

TEACH OBJECTIVE 3

All Levels: Display an outline map of North America, and distribute blank outline maps to each student. Point out the following regions to students: Arctic and Subarctic, Northwest Pacific Coast, California Coast, West and Southwest, Great Plains, Southeast, and the Northeast. Ask students to share information about the environment in each of these regions. Have students fill in their outline maps accordingly, for example, they might draw snowflakes in the Arctic region of their map. After students' maps are completed, lead a class discussion about how these different environments might influence the cultures that lived in these regions. Write students ideas on the chalkboard. To conclude, have students look up how the environment affected the culture in these regions in their textbooks to see how accurate their ideas were. **[English Language Learners]**

TEACH OBJECTIVE 4

Level 1: Make a chart on the board with the following headings: *The Far North, The Pacific Northwest, The West and Southwest, The Great Plains, The East.* Then fill in the chart with information about the cultures that lived in each of these regions. Charts should include the names of various groups, the types of houses they lived in, what they did to obtain food, and any particular difficulties they faced. **[English Language Learners]**

Level 3: Have students imagine that they are early Native American architects. Have students choose one of the culture groups whose housing is described in the chapters. Have students create a set of drawings and floormaps that might be used to construct this type of dwelling.

REVIEW AND ASSESS

Have students complete the **Sections 1** and **2 Review** questions. Then provide each student with five index cards. Have each student write five questions, one on each index card, on the content of this lesson. Tell them to write the answer on the back of the card. Finally, organize the class into pairs and ask students to quiz each other. Then have students complete **Daily Quiz 1.1** and **1.2.**

RETEACH

Have students complete **Main Idea Activities for English Language Learners and Special-Needs Students 1.1** and **1.2.** Turn the lesson objectives listed at the beginning of this lesson plan into questions. Then organize the class into four groups, assigning each group one of these questions. Have each group create a drawing or some other form of visual that answer the questions. **[English Language Learners, Cooperative Learning]**

EXTEND

Students can use the library and other resources to research information about religious ceremonies practiced in one of the culture areas of North America. Have each student write a short report focusing on these ceremonies and explaining their significance. **[Block Scheduling]**

LESSON 2

(For use with Sections 3 and 4, pages 17–22)

OBJECTIVES

1. Analyze the reasons why Vikings were able to explore new lands, and describe the significance of their voyages.

2. Examine the role of the feudal system and the Catholic Church in Europe during the Middle Ages.

3. Analyze the impact of Islam in the Mediterranean region.

4. Explain how trade influenced different regions of Asia and Africa.

LET'S GET STARTED!

Organize the class into five groups and have each group sit in a different area of the classroom. Give each group 25 of the same item, such as straws, toothpicks, or cotton balls, but be sure to give different items to each group. Explain to students that the goal of this activity is for each group to gather as many different items as they can by trading with the other groups. After a few minutes, discuss the process of trading with the class. Ask students what challenges they faced as they negotiated for different products. Conclude by telling students that in this lesson they will learn about the importance of trade during the Middle Ages.

TEACH OBJECTIVE 1

Level 1: Have students make a drawing showing what achievements allowed the Vikings to explore lands far from their home. Have students create captions for their drawings that explain the significance of Viking voyages. **[English Language Learners]**

TEACH OBJECTIVE 2

Level 2: Assign each student one of the following roles: a member of the nobility, a merchant, a monk or nun, or a peasant. Then have each student write a diary entry that describes a typical day in that person's life. Tell students that entries should include information about important aspects of society in the Middle Ages, including the Catholic Church.

Level 3: Have students analyze the influence of the Catholic Church on women in the Middle Ages. Students should write a short report describing how women benefited from the Church.

TEACH OBJECTIVE 3

Level 1: Organize the class into small groups. Tell groups to imagine they are historians contributing a chapter to a book about the Middle Ages. Have each group create an outline for a chapter that discusses the changes that took place in the late Middle Ages and the events that brought about these changes. **[English Language Learners, Cooperative Learning]**

TEACH OBJECTIVE 4

Level 1: Review with students the text about the spread of Islam, on pages 23–24, and its effect on the Mediterranean region. Then organize the class into small groups. Have each group write a short essay about whether the spread of Islam benefited the region overall or harmed it. **[English Language Learners, Cooperative Learning]**

TEACH OBJECTIVE 5

All Levels: Provide students an outline map of the world. Have students shade the African trading kingdoms, China, Europe, and areas controlled by Muslims during the Middle Ages. Then ask students to mark the trade routes that connected African traders, Chinese traders, Italian merchants, Muslims, and Vikings to other parts of the world. After students have completed their maps, lead a discussion about how these trading networks influenced people and cultures in Africa and Asia. **[English Language Learners]**

Level 3: Organize students into two groups. One group will support China's involvement in international trade, and the other group will oppose it. Have each group write an introductory statement presenting the perspective assigned to it. Remind students that these statements should refer to the reasons China originally joined in international trade and why it eventually withdrew. Then hold a debate on this topic. **[Cooperative Learning]**

REVIEW AND ASSESS

Have students complete the **Sections 3** and **4 Review** questions. Then organize students into pairs. Direct each student to create a 10-question quiz based on the information discussed in this lesson. Have students alternate quizzing their partner on the material. Then have students complete **Daily Quiz 1.3** and **1.4.**

RETEACH

Have students complete **Main Idea Activities for English Language Learners and Special-Needs Students 1.3** and **1.4.** Then organize the class into several small groups. Have groups construct a graphic organizer that summarizes the main points discussed in this lesson. **[English Language Learners]**

EXTEND

Have students use library resources or search the Internet through the HRW Go site to find information on European trade fairs. Ask them to use their findings to construct an annotated map showing where these fairs were held.

Suggest that they include in their annotations such information as when the fairs were held, what kinds of goods were traded, and what special activities took place in the towns during the fairs. Encourage students to display and discuss their maps. **[Block Scheduling]**

TEAM TEACHING STRATEGIES

Adena Culture

GOAL

In this activity, students will learn about early Native American societies in North America by creating a bulletin-board display about the Adena culture of the Ohio River valley.

PLANNING

- **Purpose** This activity may be used in combination with teacher-directed lessons, as an enrichment activity, or as a performance-based assessment of content mastery.

- **Suggested Time** Plan to spend two lesson blocks and two homework assignments on this activity. Provide time for students to present and discuss their bulletin-board displays.

- **Teaching Team** At least one social studies teacher and one language arts teacher should take part in teaching this activity.

- **Group Size** This activity works best as a small-group project. However, you may wish to assign the activity as an extra credit option for individual students.

- **Materials and Resources** Provide students with the novel *The Eyes in the Forest* by Mary Q. Steele and William O. Steele, Rubric 8: Collages, and Rubric 22: Multimedia Presentations in the *Alternative Assessment Handbook.* Have students use their textbooks, the library, and any other research materials that will help them find information about the Adena culture.

IMPLEMENTATION

1. Give students an overview of this activity by explaining that they will first study the novel *The Eye in the Forest* by Mary Q. Steele and William O. Steele. Then they will create bulletin-board displays about the Adena culture.

2. Using the text in Section 2 of the chapter, lead students in a discussion of early Native American societies in eastern and midwestern North America. Then make a brief presentation on the novel and its elements—plot, character, setting, theme, and point of view. Conclude by telling students that *The Eye in the Forest* is the story of Kontu, an Adena youth who makes a long and dangerous journey in search of the Sacred Eye, the place where his people originated.

3. Next, have students read *The Eye in the Forest.* As they read, have them sketch maps of Kontu's journey. Also, encourage them to make notes on subjects such as the physical geography of the lands where the Adena live; the religious beliefs of the Adena; and the kinds of food, clothing, and shelter the Adena use.

4. When students have completed their reading, tell groups that their task is to create a bulletin-board display titled "Kontu's Journey." Inform students that displays should be based on the sketches and notes they made during their reading of *The Eye in the Forest* and on research on Adena culture. Mention that the display should consist of an introduction that summarizes the plot of *The Eye in the Forest*, as well as illustrated and annotated maps of Kontu's journey in search of the Sacred Eye. Illustrations should include sketches of artifacts, the kinds of shelter the Adena lived in, and the foods they ate. Annotations should describe elements of the Adena way of life. Remind students that their maps need to show the major landforms and bodies of water that Kontu encounters on his journey.

5. Suggest that groups begin their task by reviewing the rubrics, which list the basic requirements for different kinds of visual displays. Finally, to ensure that all students are involved in the task, you might assign particular responsibilities to each group member. For example, one student might have overall responsibility for research, a second for artwork design, a third for writing, and so on.

6. When displays are completed, have groups exhibit them around the classroom. Conclude by holding a class discussion on whether the information in historical novels is reliable.

ASSESSMENT

1. To assess students' bulletin-board displays, use Rubric 8: Collages and Rubric 22: Multimedia Presentations in the *Alternative Assessment Handbook* or in a customizable format on the One-Stop Planner.

2. Additional grades can be based on students' participation in the concluding discussion.

The Age of Exploration

★ ★

BLOCK SCHEDULING LESSON PLANS

THINK ABOUT THEMES

Global Relations

Agree Europeans as well as Native Americans benefited from European explorations.

Disagree Native American cultures were destroyed during European exploration.

Economics

Agree Trading with other countries leads to new alliances.

Disagree Trading with other countries takes away resources needed by your own country.

Science, Techology & Society

Agree With each new invention some aspect of life is improved.

Disagree New inventions encouraged explorers to venture farther from home and safety.

LESSON 1

(For use with Sections 1 and 2, pp. 32–43)

OBJECTIVES

1. Explain how the Commercial Revolution and the Renaissance changed Europe.

2. Analyze the reasons why western Europeans sought a sea route for trade with Africa and Asia, and evaluate the consequences of early Portuguese exploration on Africans.

3. Discuss Columbus's goal, and identify what he did during his explorations in the Americas.

4. Describe Portugal's reaction to news of Columbus's voyages.

LET'S GET STARTED!

Ask students to identify technological advances that have made it easier to communicate and trade with people who live in other parts of the world. *(Students might mention inventions such as the airplane, the fax machine, the Internet, or the telephone.)* Remind the class that it was not always this easy to communicate or trade with people who lived far away. Then tell students that in this lesson they will learn how the

Commercial Revolution, the Renaissance, and exploration and trade changed Europe. They will also learn how trade and exploration affected other cultures.

TEACH OBJECTIVE 1

All Levels: Organize the class into small groups and assign each group either the Commercial Revolution or the Renaissance. Have each group create the front page of a newspaper. Front pages should consist of a headline that explains the topic, an article that discusses the changes it brought to Europe, a picture that illustrates these changes, and an editorial stating whether or not these changes were good for Europe. **[English Language Learners, Cooperative Learning]**

Level 3: Have students consider the relationship between the Commercial Revolution and the Renaissance. Then have students write an essay about whether the Renaissance would have taken place without the Commercial Revolution.

TEACH OBJECTIVE 2

All Levels: Organize the class into small groups. Have each group create a petition to send to the king of Portugal asking for the end of the slave trade. Petitions should explain the ways in which the slave trade is harming African society and explore its effects on European society. **[English Language Learners, Cooperative Learning]**

Level 3: Tell students to imagine that they are lobbyists for a group of traders in Western Europe. They have been hired to create interest among potential investors in funding an expedition to find a sea route for trade with Asia. Have each student write a sales pitch to present to potential investors, emphasizing why a new sea route is important to the European economy and how traders and merchants will profit if such a route is discovered.

TEACH OBJECTIVE 3

Level 1: Have students create images that are representative of the time Columbus spent in Hispaniola. Images might include the people he met or his activities there. Ask students to use phrases from Columbus's logbook as captions for their illustrations. **[English Language Learners]**

Level 3: Have students create a 10-entry logbook that Columbus might have written. Logbooks should start when Columbus departed Europe and should conclude upon his return. Remind students that entries should cover such topics as Columbus's goal in sailing West, the discovery of America, what he found in America, and the reaction he expected when he returned to Europe with news of his discovery.

TEACH OBJECTIVE 4

Level 2: Encourage students to imagine that they lived in Portugal around 1500. Have them write a paragraph explaining their reactions to the news of Columbus's voyage. Tell students that their paragraphs should also predict how Columbus's voyage will affect life in Western Europe.

All Levels: Encourage students to read the novel *Morning Girl* by Michael Dorris, which describes the arrival of Columbus in the New World from the viewpoint of a young Taino girl. Then have students write a short story about Columbus's actions in the Caribbean from the viewpoint of the Taino. Remind

students that their stories should include not only a description of Columbus's actions, but also the Taino's feelings about these actions. **[English Language Learners]**

REVIEW AND ASSESS

Have students complete the **Sections 1** and **2 Review** questions. Then have them create a graphic organizer that illustrates the relationships among the Commercial Revolution, the Renaissance, and European interest in exploration, expansion, and trade. Finally, have students complete **Daily Quiz 2.1** and **2.2.**

EXTEND

Have students review their textbooks to identify scientific and technological developments that helped make the Age of Exploration possible. Then have them use resources in the library to research these developments. Direct students to use their findings to write an entry for each development that might appear in a science encyclopedia. **[Block Scheduling]**

LESSON 2

(For use with Sections 3 and 4, pp. 44–53)

OBJECTIVES

1. Discuss the areas that Portugal explored and the results of these voyages.

2. Evaluate the achievements of Cabot, Vespucci, and Magellan.

3. Analyze the effects of new trade routes on Portugal and Spain.

4. Evaluate how the Columbian Exchange affected Europeans and American Indians.

5. Explain why some countries were searching for a Northwest Passage.

LET'S GET STARTED!

Ask students what they already know about early explorations of the Americas, such as early explorers, where they traveled, and why they undertook these explorations. List students' responses on the chalkboard. Tell students that in this lesson, they will learn more about early European explorations of the Americas.

TEACH OBJECTIVE 1

Level 1: Ask students to identify the areas that Vasco da Gama, and Pedro Álvares Cabral explored on a map of the world. Point out the distance between these areas and Portugal. Ask students to explain why Portugal would benefit from these explorations. **[English Language Learners]**

Level 2: Have students imagine that they are sailing with either da Gama or Cabral. Then ask students to write a letter to a friend in Portugal that explains where they are traveling, what they are seeing, and what effect their exploration will have on Europe generally and on Portugal specifically.

TEACH OBJECTIVE 2

Level 1: Provide students with outline maps of the world. Then have students trace the routes and destinations of John Cabot, Amerigo Vespucci, and Ferdinand Magellan on the maps. Tell students to create a color-coded key that assigns a color to each explorer. Use students' completed maps to lead a class discussion about the achievements of these explorers and how these achievements benefited all of Europe as well as individual European countries.
[English Language Learners]

TEACH OBJECTIVE 3

Level 1: Create a chart with three columns on the chalkboard. Place the following labels at the top of each column: *Country, How Country Established Trading Empire,* and *Land Holdings.* Under *Country,* write *Spain* and *Portugal.* Then have students provide answers to fill in the rest of the chart. Use the completed chart to lead a class discussion about how new trade routes affected Portugal and Spain. **[English Language Learners]**

TEACH OBJECTIVE 4

All Levels: Ask students to think about how the world would be different if the Europeans had not landed in the Americas when they did. Have students suggest events, developments, and consequences described in the chapter that occurred as a result of European exploration in the Americas and compare those to their speculation regarding a world in which Europeans did not land in the Americas. Write students' answers on the chalkboard. Then organize the class into small groups. Have each group write and illustrate a fable about the world today if Europeans had never landed in the Americas. Encourage students to be creative yet logical when writing their fables. Have each group present its fable to the class. **[English Language Learners, Cooperative Learning]**

Level 3: Organize a debate on the positive and negative effects of the European voyages of exploration. Encourage debaters to consider short- and long-term effects of European exploration, particularly for Europeans and Native Americans. **[Cooperative Learning]**

TEACH OBJECTIVE 5

All Levels: Divide students into pairs. Have each pair write a dialogue between an explorer and a European monarch. The explorer is asking for funding for a journey to find the Northwest Passage. The explorer should try to convince the monarch to provide funding and support, and the monarch should respond appropriately and with some skepticism. Then have pairs present their dialogues to the class. **[English Language Learners, Cooperative Learning]**

REVIEW AND ASSESS

Have students complete the **Sections 3** and **4** Review questions. Then ask students to create an annotated time line that lists and briefly summarizes the major voyages and other events discussed in Sections 3 and 4 of the chapter. Finally, have students complete **Daily Quiz 2.3** and **2.4.**

EXTEND

Have students use details in the textbooks and information gathered from the library to write a dialogue between a survivor of Magellan's circumnavigation of the world and a financial backer of the voyage. Suggest that students discuss in their dialogues the conditions endured by the crew during their journey and the significance of proving that an all-water route between Europe and Asia existed. **[Block Scheduling]**

The Age of Exploration

★ ★

TEAM TEACHING STRATEGIES

Reaching the New World

GOAL

In this activity, students will learn about Christopher Columbus's first voyage to the Americas by writing a treatment for a movie about the voyage.

PLANNING

- **Purpose**   This activity may be used in combination with teacher-directed lessons, as an enrichment activity, or as a performance-based assessment of content mastery.

- **Suggested Time**   Plan to spend two lesson blocks and two homework assignments on this activity. Provide time for students to present and discuss their movie treatments.

- **Teaching Team**   At least one social studies teacher and one language arts teacher should take part in teaching this activity.

- **Group Size**   This activity works best as a small-group project. However, you may wish to assign the activity as an extra credit option for individual students.

- **Materials and Resources**   Provide students with copies of *I Sailed with Columbus* by Susan Martin and Rubric 39 in the *Alternative Assessment Handbook*. Have students use their textbooks, the library, and any other research materials that will help them find information on Columbus's first voyage across the Atlantic.

IMPLEMENTATION

1. Give students an overview of this activity by explaining that they will first study the novel *I Sailed With Columbus* by Susan Martin. Then they will create treatments for a movie about Columbus's first voyage to the Americas.

2. Using the information under the headings "Crossing the Ocean" and "Columbus's First Explorations" on pages 39–40 as a guide, lead students in a discussion of Columbus's first voyage to the New World. Then mention that the novel that students will read, *I Sailed With Columbus*, is the story of Diego, a 14-year-old cabin boy on Columbus's ship, the Santa María.

3. Next, have students read *I Sailed With Columbus*. As they read, have students note answers to the following questions: (1) What is the book about? (You may wish to have students write a few sentences summarizing the plot.) (2) Who are the major characters in the story? (You may wish to have students write a brief biographical sketch of each.) (3) What are the major events in the story? (4) What role does Diego play in these events?

4. When students have completed their reading, tell them that their task is to write a treatment for a movie based on *I Sailed With Columbus*. Inform students that treatments should be based on the notes they made during their reading of the novel and on research on Columbus's first voyage. Mention that the treatment should consist of an introduction that summarizes the plot of the movie, an annotated list of the major events that will be covered in the movie, brief biographies of the movie's major characters, and a fully scripted scene depicting one of the listed events. Suggest that students begin by reviewing the rubric, which lists the basic requirements for writing skits and theater pieces, before they begin this last activity.

5. When students have completed their treatments, call on volunteers to present their work to the class. You may wish to have students who are working in groups perform their scripted scenes for the class. Conclude the lesson by holding a class discussion on whether or not the movies are a suitable medium for presenting historical information.

ASSESSMENT

1. To assess students' movie treatments, use the Rubric: Writing to Create in the *Alternative Assessment Handbook* or in a customizable format on the One-Stop Planner.

2. Additional grades can be based on students' participation in the concluding discussion.

THINK ABOUT THEMES

Global Relations

Agree Larger forces always have the advantage in warfare.

Disagree Superior weapons and tactics will always win a war regardless of the number of soldiers.

Geography

Agree Natural resources are the only reason for exploration.

Disagree Nations should not explore in the hopes of gaining natural resources.

Economics

Agree A colony only provides economic benefits for its mother country.

Disagree A mother country should not depend on the economic benefits of its colonies.

LESSON 1

(For use with Sections 1 and 2, pp. 66–77)

OBJECTIVES

1. Compare Hernán Cortés's conquest of the Aztec to Francisco Pizarro's conquest of the Inca in Peru.

2. Explain the reasons for Spanish exploration of Florida and the American Southwest.

3. Describe how Spain organized and governed its empire in the Americas.

4. Analyze the structure of New Spain's economy and society.

5. Explain why the Spanish settled in the borderlands.

LET'S GET STARTED!

Discuss with students how they would feel if aliens from another planet arrived in the United States. Then point out that in this lesson they will learn about how the native peoples of the Americas reacted when they first encountered the Europeans who came to explore and settle.

TEACH OBJECTIVE 1

Level 1: Have students create a compare-and-contrast chart on the Spanish conquest of the Aztec and Inca empires. Have students list the key elements of Cortés's conquest of the Aztec Empire in one column and the key elements of Pizarro's conquest of the Inca Empire in the other column. Then have students underline common elements and explain the elements that are different. **[English Language Learners]**

Level 2: Have students write a paper explaining the similarities and differences between the collapse of the Aztec and Inca empires. Ask volunteers to share their papers with the rest of the class.

TEACH OBJECTIVE 2

Level 1: List the following explorers on the chalkboard: *Juan Ponce de León, Álvar Núñez Cabez de Vaca, Hernando de Soto, Francisco Vásquez de Coronado*. Have each student choose one of these explorers and create an illustration that explains the reasons for his exploration. Students should label their illustrations with a descriptive caption that includes where the explorer traveled and when. **[English Language Learners]**

TEACH OBJECTIVE 3

All Levels: Have students create organizational charts that show how Spain organized and governed its colonies in the Americas. **[English Language Learners]**

Level 1: Have students work in small groups to create a series of commemorative stamps that illustrate how Spain organized and governed its empire in the Americas. Each group should produce four stamps representing the role of the Council of the Indies, missions, presidios, and pueblos. **[English Language Learners]**

TEACH OBJECTIVE 4

All Levels: Organize the class into small groups. Have each group imagine that they are Native Americans or enslaved Africans forced to labor for New Spain. Have each group write a short story that describes life under the *encomienda* system and on the plantations. Remind students that stories should include information about the economic system of New Spain and their place within it. **[English Language Learners, Cooperative Learning]**

Level 3: Ask students to consider problems associated with having a class system based on birthplace or race. Then have students write a newspaper editorial that describes the class system in New Spain and explains why a person who was designated as being in one of its lower classes might wish to change the system.

TEACH OBJECTIVE 5

All Levels: Have students create a graphic organizer explaining what prompted Spain to establish settlements in the borderlands. Then have students write a short paragraph related to each cause, explaining whether or not the Spanish were successful at achieving each goal. **[English Language Learners]**

REVIEW AND ASSESS

Have students complete the **Sections 1** and **2 Review** questions. Then have students write newspaper headlines on each of the lesson's objectives. Finally, have students complete **Daily Quiz 3.1** and **3.2.**

RETEACH

Have students complete **Main Idea Activities for English Language Learners and Special-Needs Students 3.1** and **3.2.** Have each student select an illustration from both Section 1 and 2. Then ask each student to write a caption for each illustration that explains its significance and ties it to the section content. **[English Language Learners]**

EXTEND

Have students list examples of Spanish influences in American culture and life today. Examples might include: animals, architectural styles, foods, place names, and plants. Then have students create a scrapbook of Spanish influences in America. **[Block Scheduling]**

LESSON 2

(For use with Sections 3 and 4, pp. 78–87)

OBJECTIVES

1. Define the Protestant Reformation and explain how it changed Europe.

2. Discuss the reasons why Spain and England went to war in the late 1500s, and analyze what led to the end of Spain's Golden Age.

3. Analyze the reasons for French, Dutch, and English interest in colonizing North America, and identify the common problems faced by French, Dutch, and Swedish colonies.

4. Describe what happened to the first English settlements in North America.

LET'S GET STARTED!

Ask students to name their school's chief rival in football and basketball. Then point out that nations also have rivalries and that these rivalries often involve territorial claims. Remind the class that Spain was the first nation to claim colonies in the Americas and that other nations wanted to join the race. Tell students that in this lesson they will be studying how England successfully challenged Spain's power in the Americas.

TEACH OBJECTIVE 1

All Levels: Have students create a flowchart illustrating the purpose and spread of the Protestant Reformation and the ways in which it changed Europe. Remind students to include key individuals and events in their flowcharts.
[English Language Learners]

TEACH OBJECTIVE 2

Level 1: Organize the class into several small groups. Have each group create a scrapbook about Spain's Golden Age. Remind each group that each entry in its scrapbook should be accompanied by an explanatory caption.
[English Language Learners, Cooperative Learning]

Level 3: Organize the class into small groups and have each group use the information in Section 3 to write a movie script about the war between Spain and England and the decline of Spain's Golden Age. Tell students that their movie scripts should have a catchy title, a plot, characters, dialogue, and stage directions. (You may wish to tell students that they can break up their script into several different scenes.) If time permits, have groups perform or videotape their movies for the class. **[Cooperative Learning]**

TEACH OBJECTIVE 3

Level 1: Provide students with an outline map of North America. Have them locate and identify on their maps the first colonies established by France, the Netherlands, and England. Suggest that students create a color-coded key that identifies the nations along with their explorers, shown on the map. Finally, ask students to write an extended caption that explains why the various nations wanted to explore and establish colonies in the Americas.
[English Language Learners]

Level 3: Have students imagine that they are American Indians observing Dutch, French, and Swedish settlers. Tell students to create an oral history explaining the actions of these newcomers and the problems they faced in North America. Encourage volunteers to share their oral histories with the class.

TEACH OBJECTIVE 4

Level 2: Have students create an annotated time line about the first English settlements in North America. Timelines should include the dates of each of their selected events, a brief description of the events' significance, and an image or map for at least half of the events.

Level 3: Discuss with students what happened to the first English settlements in North America. Then organize the class into small groups. Tell each group they are creating a documentary about these events. Have groups create a set of storyboards that show what information they will include in their documentaries. Tell students to end their documentaries with their own theories about what happened to the English settlers at Roanoke.
[Cooperative Learning]

REVIEW AND ASSESS

Have students complete the **Sections 3** and **4 Review** questions. Then have students create an outline of the important events and people in **Sections 3** and **4**. Finally, have students complete **Daily Quiz 3.3** and **3.4**.

RETEACH

Have students complete **Main Idea Activities for English Language Learners and Special-Needs Students 3.3** and **3.4**. Find examples of pictures that show the reasons for the Reformation, the decline of Spain, European settlement of North America, and the conditions these settlers faced. For example, find a picture of Martin Luther (the Reformation), pictures of people fishing (reason for settlement), or snow (conditions faced). Use these pictures and drawings of the flags of each country discussed in this section to create a matching activity. Assist students with matching each country's flag to the conditions faced by its settlers and the reasons for its decision to colonize North America. **[English Language Learners]**

EXTEND

Organize students into groups and assign each group one of the following topics: (1) the Reformation; (2) the defeat of the Spanish Armada; (3) the decline of Spain; (4) the French, Dutch, or Swedish colonies in North America; (5) early English settlements in North America. Have each group create a graphic organizer that explains the relationships in their assigned topic. Have a representative from each group present their graphic organizer to the class. **[Block Scheduling]**

European Settlements in North America

GOAL

In this activity, students will learn more about early European settlement in North America by writing journal entries from the viewpoint of a Dutch, English, French, or Swedish settler.

PLANNING

- **Purpose**   This activity may be used in combination with teacher-directed lessons, as an enrichment activity, or as a performance-based assessment of content mastery.

- **Suggested Time**   Plan to spend two lesson blocks and one homework assignment on this activity. Provide time for students to offer each other feedback on their finished journals.

- **Teaching Team**   At least one social studies teacher and one language arts teacher should take part in teaching this activity.

- **Group Size**   This activity works best as an individual assignment. However, students may work in small groups to undertake research.

- **Materials and Resources**   Provide students with copies of *The Writings of Junípero Serra*. You might also provide students with copies of the Rubric 15: Journals in the *Alternative Assessment Handbook*. Have students use their textbooks to help them locate information about early European settlement in North America.

IMPLEMENTATION

1. Give students an overview of the activity by explaining that they will learn more about European settlement in the Americas by first reading excerpts from the journal of a Spanish settler. Then they will write journal entries from the viewpoint of a settler from England, France, the Netherlands, or Sweden.

2. Using the text for Section 4 of the chapter as a guide, lead students in a discussion of early European settlement in North America. Focus the discussion on why people from England, France, the Netherlands, and Sweden came to North America. Emphasize the ways in which these people reacted to their new surroundings and how they interacted with American Indians.

3. Distribute copies of the excerpt from Junípero Serra's journal and the rubric to students. Continue by working through the excerpt with students, asking them to think about the following questions as they read: What physical features of the landscape does Serra mention? What qualities does Serra seem to be looking for in the landscape? Why do you think he is looking for these qualities? How does Serra view the American Indians he meets? As students discuss these points, encourage them to take notes.

4. Next, review the rubric with students, pointing out that it lists the basic requirements for writing a good journal. Then ask students to write a journal of a journey through an area of North America explored or settled by the Dutch, English, French, or Swedish. Remind them that they need to write the journal from the viewpoint of a traveler. Suggest that they explore such topics as the landscape, what the land might be used for, the ways of life of the Native Americans they encounter, and how these ways of life compare to European ways.

5. Call on volunteers to read their journals to the class. Use these readings as a starting point for a discussion on the usefulness of personal journals as a tool of historical research.

ASSESSMENT

1. To assess students' journals, use the Rubric 15: Journals in the *Alternative Assessment Handbook* or in a customizable format on the One-Stop Planner.

2. Additional grades can be based on students' participation in the concluding discussion.

The English Colonies

★ ★

BLOCK SCHEDULING LESSON PLANS

THINK ABOUT THEMES

Geography

Agree Cooperative weather ensures a successful harvest.

Disagree Through hard work and determination, people can overcome geographical hardships and be successful.

Economics

Agree A colony must have money to meet its basic needs.

Disagree A colony that provides for its basic needs will survive.

Culture

Agree The new colonies would not have survived without religious freedom.

Disagree Religious freedom should be fought for at all costs.

LESSON 1

(For use with Sections 1 and 2, pp. 92–102)

OBJECTIVES

1. Explain why people in England were interested in founding Jamestown and how the Jamestown colonists interacted with the local American Indians.

2. Describe the development of Virginia's plantation system and the role indentured servants and enslaved Africans played in Virginia's economy.

3. Explain why the Pilgrims came to America.

4. Define the Mayflower Compact and explain why it was important.

5. Describe life in the Plymouth colony.

LET'S GET STARTED!

Ask students to speculate on why people might be willing to leave their homeland to start a new life in a strange country thousands of miles away. *(Answers will vary but students might suggest the desire for better economic opportunities, a chance for a better life for their families, or more freedom.)* Then tell students that in this lesson they will learn about two groups of colonists who

came to North America, why they came, and what they found there.

TEACH OBJECTIVE 1

Level 1: Read aloud with students the passage from the Virginia Company advertisement under the heading "Settlement in Jamestown" (page 93 of the textbook). Discuss with students what types of people this advertisement would appeal to and what these people would hope to find in America. **[English Language Learners]**

Level 2: Have students write a short story from the viewpoint of Pocahontas or Squanto that tells about interactions between the English colonists and the local American Indians. Ask volunteers to read their stories to the rest of the class.

TEACH OBJECTIVE 2

Level 2: Write the following on the chalkboard: *wealthy colonists, indentured servants, enslaved Africans.* Ask students to write a few sentences describing the role that each group played in the development of Virginia's plantation system and economy. Have volunteers share their descriptions with the class, then lead a discussion about the economic and social interactions between these three groups.

TEACH OBJECTIVE 3

Level 1: Have students use a map to trace the journey taken by the Pilgrims from England to America. Ask students to annotate their maps to explain why the Pilgrims decided to start a new colony in America. **[English Language Learners]**

TEACH OBJECTIVE 4

All Levels: Organize students into several groups. Tell group members to imagine that they are exhibit teams working for historical museums. Their task is to design a brochure for a museum exhibit on the importance of the Mayflower Compact. Brochures should include information on who signed the compact and why their actions were significant. Have groups display their brochures for the rest of the class. **[English Language Learners, Cooperative Learning]**

TEACH OBJECTIVE 5

Level 2: Organize the class into several groups and inform them that their task is to draw up outlines for short plays, titled *Plymouth Scenes*, on life in the Plymouth Colonies. Point out that plays should consist of five or six scenes. For each scene, have groups compose a title, identify where the scene takes place, list the characters involved, and write a brief synopsis of the script. As a guide, you might mention that Plymouth scenes should cover such topics as why the Pilgrims came to North America, the establishment of Plymouth Colony, relations with American Indians, and daily life in the Plymouth community. Call on groups to present and discuss their play outlines. **[Cooperative Learning]**

REVIEW AND ASSESS

Have students complete the **Sections 1** and **2 Review** questions. Then have them create two concept webs. One web should have *Virginia Colony* at the center, while the other should have *Plymouth Colony* at the center. Strands from each web should explain why colonists came to North America, problems they faced in founding the colonies, how they made a living, how the colonies were governed, and daily life in the colonies. Then have students complete **Daily Quiz 4.1** and **4.2.**

RETEACH

Have students complete **Main Idea Activities for English Language Learners and Special-Needs Students 4.1** and **4.2.** Then have students work in small groups to write sentences using each of the Define and Identify words listed in Section 1 Review and Section 2 Review. Direct them to replace each key term or person's name with a blank space. Pair groups and have partnered groups exchange their sentences. Then ask groups to complete the sentences and return them to their authors for grading. **[English Language Learners]**

EXTEND

Ask students to imagine that it is possible for them to conduct and interview with a woman colonist in Plymouth. Have them work in pairs to create an interview that analyzes the role of women in the Pilgrim society at Plymouth. Encourage students to present their interviews to the class. **[Block Scheduling]**

LESSON 2

(For use with Sections 3 and 4, pp. 103–15)

OBJECTIVES

1. Explain the Great Migration and why it occurred.

2. Describe the role that religion and the church played in the Massachusetts Bay Colony, and discuss how the Puritans responded to dissenters.

3. Discuss the role religion played in the founding of Maryland.

4. Explain how the Carolinas were established and how their economies developed.

5. Describe how the middle colonies were founded.

LET'S GET STARTED!

Write the term *New England* on the chalkboard, and ask students what the term means to them. *(Some students might suggest an area of the northeastern United States. Other students might suggest the city of Boston. Still others might suggest such historical connections as the Pilgrims, the Puritans, and the Salem witch trials.)* Then tell students that in this lesson they will learn about the development of the New England colonies. Add that they also will learn how English colonies eventually occupied the coastal areas of North America from New England all the way south to present-day Georgia.

TEACH OBJECTIVE 1

All Levels: Ask students to imagine that they are one of the English colonists who came to America during the Great Migration. Have students write a letter to a friend back in England, explaining why they chose to leave England. **[English Language Learners]**

TEACH OBJECTIVE 2

Level 2: Discuss with students how the Puritans treated dissenters within their community. Then have students create a compare-and-contrast chart explaining the Puritans treatment of Roger Williams and Anne Hutchinson.

Level 3: Remind students that the United States values the separation of church and state, or religion and government. Tell students that was not the case in the Massachusetts Bay Colony. Have students write a short essay describing how religion influenced all aspects of life—such as education, family, and government—in the colony.

TEACH OBJECTIVE 3

Level 2: Encourage students to think about the role religion played in the founding and development of Maryland. Then ask them to create a biographical sketch of a person who might choose to settle in this colony.

TEACH OBJECTIVES 3, 4, AND 5

Level 1: Help students construct a chart to assist them in organizing information about the New England, Middle, and Southern Colonies. On the chalkboard, draw a chart with the following vertical column-headings: *Maryland Colonies, Middle Colonies,* and *the Carolinas.* Then add the following horizontal column-headings: *Colonies, When and Why Founded, Government, Religion and Education,*

Economy, and *Other Significant Information.* Ask students to copy and complete the chart by using information found in Sections 3 and 4 of their textbooks. Using the chart as a starting point, lead a discussion comparing and contrasting the New England, middle, and southern colonies. **[English Language Learners]**

Level 2: Organize the class into three groups and assign each group either Maryland, the middle colonies, or the Carolinas. Tell each group that its task is to create an illustrated time line that traces major events in the development of its assigned colony or colonial region from its founding to the 1700s. Ask each group to select at least ten important events that occurred in or to its assigned colony or colonial region and create illustrations of and annotations for these events. Then have each group construct a time line from the founding of its assigned colony or colonial region to the 1700s, placing illustrations at appropriate points. **[English Language Learners, Cooperative Learning]**

Level 3: Have students write a short report comparing and contrasting Maryland, the Carolinas, and the middle colonies. Tell students that their reports should examine such things as the founding of the colony, the population, educational opportunities, labor, crops, and religious tolerance. Ask students to include appropriate illustrations in their reports.

TEACH OBJECTIVE 4

Level 1: Remind students that North and South Carolina were originally one colony. Ask students to think about the differences that developed between the northern and southern regions of Carolina. Then have them draw two illustrations: one illustration should depict a typical scene of economic life in North Carolina and the other illustration should depict a typical scene of economic life in South Carolina. **[English Language Learners]**

CLOSE

Have each student select a colony discussed in this section. Then have them prepare a picture postcard with a message to a friend or relative in England that briefly describes a migrant's experience in the colony and the items for which the colony is known. "Send" the postcards to other members of the class, and invite comments by the recipient on the accuracy of the picture and its message.

REVIEW AND ASSESS

Have students complete the **Sections 3** and **4 Review** questions. Then have each student select one of the individuals discussed in the sections. Ask each student to write a eulogy for his or her assigned individual that describes his or her contributions to the establishment of the English colonies in North America. Direct students not to mention the names of their assigned individuals. Ask volunteers to read their eulogy to the class and have other students identify the historical figure it describes. Then have students complete **Daily Quiz 4.3** and **4.4.**

RETEACH

Have students complete **Main Idea Activities for English Language Learners and Special-Needs Students 4.3** and **4.4.** Then organize students into small groups and have each group write 10 true/false statements based on the lesson content. Ask group representatives to read statements to the class and have class members identify them as true or false. Then have students recast false statements to make them correct. **[English Language Learners]**

EXTEND

Have students use library resources to find information about the trial of Anne Hutchinson or the Salem witch trials. Then have students work in small groups to use their findings to develop a "You Are There" radio newscast on one of the two subjects. Encourage group members to read their newscasts to the class. **[Block Scheduling]**

The English Colonies

★ ★

TEAM TEACHING STRATEGIES

Colonial Graphic Novels

GOAL

In this activity, students will learn about the founding of Plymouth colony by creating short graphic novels that illustrate events in its early history.

PLANNING

- **Purpose** This activity may be used in combination with teacher-directed lessons, as an enrichment activity, or as a performance-based assessment of content mastery.

- **Suggested Time** Plan to spend two lesson blocks and one homework assignment on this activity. Provide time for students to share their graphic novels.

- **Teaching Team** At least one social studies teacher and one language arts teacher should take part in teaching this activity.

- **Group Size** Creating graphic novels works best as a small-group project. However, you may choose to assign the activity as an extra credit option for individual students.

- **Materials and Resources** Have students use their textbooks and library resourses to help them find information about the voyage of the *Mayflower* and the Pilgrims' first year at Plymouth colony. Provide students with copies of *Pilgrim Voices: Our First Year in the New World* edited by Connie and Peter Roop.

IMPLEMENTATION

1. Give students an overview of the activity by explaining that they will first read the book *Pilgrim Voices: Our First Year in the New World* edited by Connie and Peter Roop. They will then create short graphic novels illustrating events that took place during the first year of Plymouth colony. Inform students that a graphic novel shows action and events in a series of annotated pictures, rather than with continuous text.

2. Lead students in a discussion about the development of Plymouth colony. Have students make special note of the problems the Pilgrims faced in their first months in North America and how American Indians helped them face these challenges. Then mention that the book they will read, uses excerpts from diaries and journals to tell the story of the voyage of the *Mayflower* and the hardships the Pilgrims faced in their new homeland.

3. Next, have students read *Pilgrim Voices: Our First Year in the New World*. As they read, have students consider and note answers to the following questions: What was the journey across the Atlantic Ocean like? How and why did the Pilgrims select Plymouth as the site for their settlement? What challenges and hardships did they face during their first winter in North America? How did American Indians help the Pilgrims overcome these hardships?

4. When students have completed their reading, direct the groups to create a short graphic novel that illustrates some of the events related in *Pilgrim Voices: Our First Year in the*

New World. Recommend that they illustrate such events as the journey across the Atlantic, the search for a suitable location for their settlement, the Pilgrims' first meeting with American Indians, and the first Thanksgiving. Remind students that the content of their graphic novels should be based on the notes they made during class discussions, on their reading of the book, and on any research they conducted.

5. Call on volunteers to display and discuss their graphic novels. Conclude by leading students in a discussion of the reasons why the Plymouth colony was able to survive and, in time, flourish.

ASSESSMENT

1. To assess students' graphic novels, use the Rubric 3: Artwork in the *Alternative Assessment Handbook* or in a customizable format on the One-Stop Planner.

2. Additional grades can be based on students' participation in the concluding discussion.

THINK ABOUT THEMES

Economics

Agree Colonies should be required to provide economic benefits to their homeland.

Disagree Colonies are economically independent and should not be indebted to their mother country.

Geography

Agree Natural resources are the key to a successful colony.

Disagree A colony's success depends on the resourcefulness of the settlers.

Science, Technology & Society

Agree All scientific discoveries have benefited society.

Disagree Scientific discoveries benefit some people more than others.

LESSON 1

(For use with Sections 1 and 2, pp. 120–30)

lesson they will learn how people living in the British colonies experienced similar problems.

OBJECTIVES

1. Explain how representative government developed in the colonies and how the colonists influenced the rulings of colonial courts.

2. Evaluate how the Dominion of New England affected the New England colonies and how the English Bill of Rights influenced colonists.

3. Describe the effects the Navigation Acts had on the colonies' economy and the types of trade that took place in the 1700s.

4. Analyze why the colonies participated in the slave trade.

LET'S GET STARTED!

Ask students to imagine that they are members of the Triple A sports team. Triple A has to play a series of games against the Top Notch team. Top Notch management sets the rules, and changes them every so often without consulting the Triple A team. Ask students how they might feel in this situation. Tell students that in this

TEACH OBJECTIVE 1

All Levels: Organize students into groups and tell groups that they are on the editorial board of a children's magazine. Their task is to develop a plan for a special edition of the magazine that deals with government in the colonies from 1650 to 1750. The magazine will focus on the development of representative government in the colonies and colonists' influence on colonial courts. Inform groups that their plans should include a list of three articles, a brief synopsis of the content of each article, and several suggestions for illustrations for the articles. **[English Language Learners, Cooperative Learning]**

TEACH OBJECTIVE 2

Level 1: Write the following headings on the chalkboard: *James II, the Dominion of New England, the English Bill of Rights.* Then have students explain the different ways that each heading affected and influenced the New England colonists. List students' ideas on the chart. **[English Language Learners]**

TEACH OBJECTIVE 3

Level 1: Remind students of Sir William Berkeley's statement that the Navigation Acts were "mighty and destructive" to the New England economy. Ask students how these acts limited the colonial economy. Write students' answers on the chalkboard. Then lead the class in a discussion about how accurate they think Berkeley's statement was. **[English Language Learners]**

Level 2: Have students create annotated maps showing a typical voyage of a ship involved in the triangular trade. Annotations should include the goods carried and the types of trades involved.

TEACH OBJECTIVE 4

Level 2: Have students write a monologue from the perspective of a prisoner on board a slave ship during the middle passage. Monologues should explain why the colonies are participating in the slave trade. Encourage students to have their character describe the sights, sounds, and smells of the ship in their monologue, as well.

REVIEW AND ASSESS

Have students complete the **Sections 1** and **2 Review** questions. Then organize students into pairs and have partners take turns quizzing each other on the review questions. Finally, have students complete **Daily Quiz 5.1** and **5.2**. **[English Language Learners]**

RETEACH

Have students complete **Main Idea Activities for English Language Learners and Special-Needs Students 5.1** and **5.2**. Then have students list the main headings for Sections 1 and 2 of the chapter, leaving space between each entry. Copy the list and distribute it to each student. Ask students to outline Sections 1 and 2 by adding subheadings and supporting details to the list. **[English Language Learners]**

EXTEND

Refer students to the Let's Get Started! activity and their discussion about playing in a game where the other person set—and sometimes changed—the rules. Then have students work individually or in groups to list examples of how Britain set and changed the rules on the ways in which colonial governments and trade should be run. Ask students to write a personal response to Britain's actions. **[Block Scheduling]**

LESSON 2

(For use with Sections 3, 4, and 5, pp. 131–44)

OBJECTIVES

1. Explain why enslaved Africans were the main workforce in the southern colonies.

2. Identify the economic activities of the New England, Southern, and middle colonies, describing similarities and differences.

3. Analyze the message of the Great Awakening and its influence on colonial religious organizations and leaders, as well as society.

4. Explain how both the Scientific Revolution and the Enlightenment reflected new ways of thinking.

5. Describe education during colonial times.

6. Identify Benjamin Franklin's achievements as well as the contributions other colonists made to American culture in the 1700s.

LET'S GET STARTED!

Lead a discussion about the ways that the environment, including geography and climate, influences the way we live. Focus students' attention on economic activities. Then have students consider whether the geographic area where people live might influence how they think and what they believe. Tell students that in this lesson they will learn how geography affected economic activities in the colonies. They will also learn about the Great Awakening and developments in American culture.

TEACH OBJECTIVE 1

Level 1: Ask students to illustrate the types of work and tasks that enslaved Africans performed in the southern colonies. Have volunteers present their illustrations to the class. Then discuss with students the importance of enslaved Africans to the economy of the southern colonies. **[English Language Learners]**

TEACH OBJECTIVE 2

Level 1: Assign each student one of the following regions: New England colonies, middle colonies, and southern colonies. Have students create picture postcards for their assigned region. Encourage them to depict on their postcards the geography, climate, and economic activities. Ask volunteers to explain their postcards to the class. **[English Language Learners]**

Level 3: Assign students one of the following regions: New England, middle colonies, or southern colonies. Have students use their textbook or the library to find information about their assigned region. Have them use this information to write an encyclopedia entry about their regions. Entries should include such information as the population, type of economy, weather, educational opportunities, sources of labor, and religious affiliations. Ask volunteers to share their entries with the class. Then lead a discussion comparing and contrasting the three regions.

TEACH OBJECTIVE 3

Level 1: Create a chart on the chalkboard with the following headings: *Religious Groups, Religious Leaders, Women, Poor People.* Have the class work together to fill in the chart with ways that each of these groups were affected by the Great Awakening. After the chart is completed, lead a class discussion on the implications these changes might have for colonial society and politics. **[English Language Learners]**

Level 3: Ask students to consider the Great Awakening and the approaches that people took to the revival of religious sentiment. Assign the perspective of "New Light" or "Old Light" to each student. Then have students use information from their textbooks to prepare a short speech in which they identify individuals

prominent in their assigned perspective and explain the message these individuals were trying to advance.

TEACH OBJECTIVE 4

Level 2: On the chalkboard, draw four columns with the following headings: *Artists, Philosophers, Scientists,* and *Writers.* Ask students to review the section to generate a list of people who were influential during the Scientific Revolution and the Enlightenment. Write students' responses under the appropriate category on the chalkboard. Organize the class into groups of two or three and assign each group one of the names on the chalkboard. Ask each group to prepare a series of stamps commemorating the historic figure. Tell them that under each stamp they must explain the achievements of the individual featured on the stamp and how the individual reflected new ways of thinking. **[Cooperative Learning]**

TEACH OBJECTIVE 5

Level 2: Pair students. Assign one member of each pair the role of a student receiving an education in New England, and the other member of the pair the role of a student receiving an education in the southern or middle colonies. Ask students to create a dialogue in which they compare education in these regions. Ask for volunteers to present their dialogues to the class. **[Cooperative Learning]**

TEACH OBJECTIVE 6

Level 1: Reread the text under the heading "Colonial Writers and Artists" on page 144 with the class. Then ask students to write a few statements summarizing American culture in the 1700s. Remind students to think about the different art forms discussed in their textbook. Ask volunteers to share their statements. **[English Language Learners]**

Level 2: Have students write a short biography of Ben Franklin. Tell students to include an illustration with their biography.

REVIEW AND ASSESS

Have students complete the **Sections 3, 4,** and **5 Review** questions. Then organize the class into small groups and have each group create "study cards" on cultural, economic, and religious life in the colonies. Each group should develop three to five cards for each of the three geographical regions—southern colonies, middle colonies, and New England. Have group members write the question on one side of a card and answer on the other. Then have groups take turns quizzing each other on colonial economic and religious life. Finally, have students complete **Daily Quiz 5.3, 5.4** and **5.5. [English Language Learners]**

RETEACH

Have students complete **Main Idea Activities for English Language Learners and Special-Needs Students 5.3, 5.4,** and **5.5.** Then organize the class into six groups and assign each group one of the objectives for Section 3, 4, or 5. Have groups write 5 to 10 true/false statements based on the content of their Focus question. Ask group representatives to read statements to the class, and have class members identify them as true or false. Have students recast false statements to make them correct. **[English Language Learners]**

EXTEND

Organize students into groups and have group members imagine that they live in colonial America. Tell groups that have been given the task of putting together a time capsule that will show people in the future what the society, economy, and culture of colonial America was like. Tell students that the time capsule should contain 10 to 12 items and that each item should be accompanied by a note card that explains the item's significance to colonial culture. **[Block Scheduling]**

★ ★

TEAM TEACHING STRATEGIES

A Slave Ship's Log

GOAL

In this activity, students will learn about the Atlantic slave trade and the Middle Passage by writing a journal from the viewpoint of a slave on a ship making the journey from Africa to the Americas.

PLANNING

- **Purpose** This activity may be used in combination with teacher-directed lessons, as an enrichment activity, or as a performance-based assessment of content mastery.

- **Suggested Time** Plan to spend one lesson block and one homework assignment on this activity. Provide time for students to read aloud and discuss their ship's logs.

- **Teaching Team** At least one social studies teacher and one language arts teacher should take part in teaching this activity.

- **Group Size** This activity works best as an individual assignment. However, students may work in small groups to undertake research.

- **Materials and Resources** Provide students with copies of *The Atlantic Slave Trade*. You might also provide students with copies of Rubric 37: Writing Assignments and Rubric 40: Writing to Describe in the *Alternative Assessment Handbook*. Have students use their text-books to help them gather information about the Atlantic slave trade.

IMPLEMENTATION

1. Give students an overview of the activity by explaining that they will first read an excerpt about the Middle Passage from *The Interesting Narrative of the Life of Olaudah Equiano, or Gustavus Vassa, the African, Written by Himself.* Then they will write a journal of a journey from Africa to the Americas from the viewpoint of a slave aboard the ship.

2. Using the information in the text under the heading "The Middle Passage" in Section 2 of the chapter as a guide, lead students in a discussion of the Atlantic slave trade. Have students make particular note of the conditions the enslaved Africans endured during the Middle Passage.

3. Distribute copies of the excerpt from Equiano's autobiography and the rubrics to students. Provide students with the following biographical information on Equiano:

    Olaudah Equiano was born around 1745 in the Kingdom of Benin in present-day southern Nigeria. Until he was captured at the age of 10, he did not know of the existence of the ocean or of white people. As a slave, he worked on plantations in the West Indies and in Virginia. He also fought for the British in the French and Indian War, and served as a sailor aboard the ships of a West Indian merchant. In 1766 Equiano purchased his freedom. Some 10 years later he settled in England and devoted his life to the antislavery movement.

Continue by working through the excerpt with students, asking them to consider the following as they read: What were conditions like for the enslaved Africans aboard the ship? How did the enslaved Africans respond to these conditions? If the enslaved Africans were potentially a profitable "cargo," why did the slave traders treat them so badly? Encourage students to take notes as they read.

4. Have students create a journal from the perspective of a slave on board a slave ship during the middle passage. Have students base their ship's logs on notes taken during class discussions, the reading of the Equiano excerpt, and any research on the Atlantic slave trade that they have undertaken. Encourage students to use imagery when describing the sights, sounds, and smells of the ship. Point out that Rubric 40: Writing to Describe should prove useful in completing this task.

5. Have students share their completed journals with the rest of the class. Then remind students that Equiano used his experiences as a slave to further the cause of the anti-slavery movement. Conclude by asking students to discuss how the information contained in their ship's logs might be used as a tool by abolitionists.

ASSESSMENT

1. To assess students' ship's logs, use Rubric 37: Writing Assignments and Rubric 40: Writing to Describe in the *Alternative Assessment Handbook* or in a customizable format on the One-Stop Planner.

2. Additional grades can be based on students' participation in the concluding discussion.

THINK ABOUT THEMES

Global Relations

Agree Colonies should always support their homeland.

Disagree Colonies are not bound to fight the enemies of their mother country.

Geography

Agree Nations always compete with each other for land and territory.

Disagree A nation's expansion or growth never infringes on another nation's territory.

Economics

Agree Lack of representation is the price people must pay in order to be well protected.

Disagree Protection from enemies is a right, not a privilege, and people should not have to sacrifice representation for it.

LESSON 1

(For use with Sections 1 and 2, pp. 158–66)

OBJECTIVES

1. Describe how the English colonists and American Indians viewed each other.

2. Identify wars that the English colonists fought against other European colonists, and explain how the French and Indian War affected the British colonies.

3. Explain why many colonists moved onto the frontier.

4. Identify the factors leading to Pontiac's Rebellion.

5. Describe the Proclamation of 1763, and analyze its effectiveness.

LET'S GET STARTED!

Ask students to identify the reasons why Europeans began to establish colonies in the Americas. Explain that when European settlement began in the Americas, it caused problems between American Indians and colonists, and among European nations. Inform students that these problems ultimately led to a series of wars.

Tell students that in this lesson they will learn about these wars and the effects they had on colonies in North America.

TEACH OBJECTIVE 1

All Levels: Have students create a chart that shows the relationship between the different groups living on the frontier and in the back-country. Suggest that students use *English Colonists* and *French Colonists* as the vertical headings and *Trade with American Indians* and *Conflicts with American Indians* as the horizontal headings. Ask students to fill in the chart with details about each category. Conclude the lesson by reviewing students' charts with the class. **[English Language Learners]**

TEACH OBJECTIVE 2

Level 2: Have students imagine that they were a soldier who marched with General Braddock. Then ask them write a journal entry describing their defeat at Fort Duquesne. Journal entries should talk about the fort's history and role in the French and Indian War.

Level 3: Organize the class into two groups and assign each group either Queen Anne's War or the French and Indian War. Have groups use their textbooks to gather information about their topic. Then have them use this information to make a list that summarizes the causes and results of their assigned conflict. Give each group several pieces of posterboard, and instruct them to create a plan for a Web site that outlines the history of their assigned topic. Encourage students to create charts, graphs, maps, or articles that provide further information. Tell each group to design its Web page so that it contains links to other Web pages about the subject as well as Web pages about other wars that the French and English colonists fought. Conclude by having each group explain the causes and results of its assigned conflict and the design of their Web page. **[Cooperative Learning]**

TEACH OBJECTIVE 3

Level 2: Give students a blank outline map that features the eastern half of the United States. Then have students annotate their maps with words and pictures that show why settlers moved onto the frontier.

TEACH OBJECTIVE 4

Level 2: Have students write a biographical sketch about Pontiac. Sketches should focus on why he wanted to drive the white settlers out of the Ohio River Valley. Ask students to include an image of chief Pontiac interacting with the other American Indians.

All Levels: Organize the class into small groups. Have groups use their textbooks to find information on Pontiac's Rebellion. Direct the groups to use their findings to create the front page of a newspaper with a story about war. Remind students to include a headline, a cover story that describes the war, illustrations or maps that highlight significant aspects of the war, the name of the newspaper, and the newspaper's publication date. **[English Language Learners, Cooperative Learning]**

TEACH OBJECTIVE 5

Level 1: Write a two-column chart on the chalkboard with the following headings: *American Indians' Point of View* and *Settlers' Point of View.* Ask students why the American Indians and the settlers might have held different points of view

with regard to the Proclamation of 1763. Then fill in the chart with the class. Under the first heading, list reasons why the Americans Indians might like the proclamation. Under the second heading, list reasons why white settlers might oppose the proclamation. **[English Language Learners]**

Level 3: Tell students to imagine that they are journalists living in the Ohio River Valley in the late 1760s. Have each student write a newspaper editorial analyzing the effectiveness of the Proclamation of 1763. Editorials should include reasons the Proclamation was issued, how white settlers reacted to it, as well as a personal reaction on the part of the writer.

REVIEW AND ASSESS

Have students complete the **Sections 1** and **2 Review** questions. Then have them develop graphic organizers that show cause and effects of the French and Indian War and Pontiac's Rebellion. Have students share their graphic organizers with the class. Then have students complete **Daily Quiz 6.1** and **6.2.**

RETEACH

Have students complete **Main Idea Activities for English Language Learners and Special-Needs Students 6.1** and **6.2.** Then ask students to think about the relations between English colonists and American Indians. Ask students to write a one- or two-paragraph description of the problems between the two groups and how these problems led to war. Ask volunteers to share their paragraphs with the class. **[English Language Learners]**

EXTEND

Have students use the library and other resourses to find information on one of the American Indian groups mentioned in Sections 1 or 2. Then have students use this information to create a mural about some aspect of that group's life. For example, students might create a mural about an important ritual or ceremony for their group. **[Block Scheduling]**

LESSON 2

(For use with Sections 3 and 4, pp. 167–75)

OBJECTIVES

1. Explain why Great Britain created new taxes for the colonies, explore the reasons colonists disliked them, and analyze the ways that colonists challenged them.

2. Describe colonists' responses to the Townshend Acts.

3. Analyze why the Boston Massacre and the Boston Tea Party were significant events.

4. Explain the purpose of the Intolerable Acts.

LET'S GET STARTED!

Write the following terms on the chalkboard: *boycotts, hunger strikes, marches, petitions, rallies, sit-ins,* and *strikes.* Then ask students to identify what these terms have in common. *(Students' answers might be that they are all forms of peaceful protest.)* Lead a class discussion about these peaceful forms of protest, and give examples of successful protests that have used these methods. Then tell students that sometimes these peaceful methods do not achieve a group's desired goal. When peaceful protests go unanswered, people sometimes resort to the destruction of property and threats of violence. Tell students that in this lesson they will learn that American colonists generally followed this pattern when protesting taxes imposed by the British government.

TEACH OBJECTIVE 1

Level 1: Ask students to explain why Great Britain created new taxes for the colonies, and write their answers on the board. Ask students to name specific taxes, and list these on the board. Then create a flow chart showing the progress of new taxation. Close by leading a discussion about how colonists reacted to these taxes. **[English Language Learners]**

All Levels: Organize the class into small groups. Have group members imagine that they are living in the colonies in the 1760s. Have each group discuss their options regarding the new taxes (pay the tax, protest and pay the tax, refuse to pay, boycott British goods, or destroy British goods.) Tell groups to make a list of the arguments for and against each option and to vote on which method they would prefer to use. Then have groups create a broadside announcing how the colonies should respond to Britain's new taxes. **[English Language Learners, Cooperative Learning]**

TEACH OBJECTIVE 2

Level 1: Have students draw an illustration showing the colonists' response to the Townshend Acts. Ask students to include a caption with their illustration. **[English Language Learners]**

Level 3: Have students imagine that they are members of the Sons of Liberty or the Daughters of Liberty. Have each student write a speech to give to the colonists about the course of action the colonists ought to take in order to protest the Townshend Acts. Ask volunteers to read their speeches to the class.

TEACH OBJECTIVE 3

Level 3: Have students imagine that they lived in Boston from 1770 to 1774. Then have each student write a journal entry in which he or she describes the most significant events that took place during this period. Students' journal entries should explain the causes of the events they reported and the colonists' feelings about them. Ask volunteers to share their journal entries with the class.

TEACH OBJECTIVE 4

Level 1: Divide the class into two groups. Tell one group to imagine that they are British citizens living in England and the other group to imagine that they are American colonists. Then direct students' attention to the listing of the Intolerable Acts under the heading "The Intolerable Acts" in Section 4 of their textbook. Read each law aloud. Ask the group of British citizens why Parliament included this law. Then ask the group of American colonists why this law made them angry. **[English Language Learners, Cooperative Learning]**

Level 3: Remind students that Parliament responded to the Boston Tea Party by passing the Coercive Acts. Tell students that Parliament found these acts to be justified based on the colonists' previous actions but that the colonists found them intolerable. Have half the class write a two-paragraph editorial that might have been written by a British citizen who supported the government's policy toward the colonies. Have the other half of the class write an editorial that might have been written by an American colonist who opposed the British government's colonial policies.

REVIEW AND ASSESS

Have students complete the **Sections 3** and **4 Review** questions. Assign each student a partner and ask each pair to write the Define and Identify words from these sections on small slips of paper. Ask partners to take turns choosing a slip of paper and making statements about the significance of the term. For example, a student who has chosen the term *Sugar Act* may describe it as a tax on sugar that was imposed to help the British pay for a standing army in the colonies. Then have students complete **Daily Quiz 6.3** and **6.4.**

RETEACH

Have students complete **Main Idea Activities for English Language Learners and Special-Needs Students 6.3** and **6.4.** Then organize students into groups of five. Give each group a large sheet of paper on which is drawn the outline of a flowchart of events titled *British Actions and Colonial Responses, 1767–1774.* Group members should take turns filling in the chart. When groups have finished, ask volunteers to present their flowcharts to the class. **[English Language Learners, Cooperative Learning]**

EXTEND

Have students imagine that they are part of a rally protesting Britain's implementation of the Stamp Act, the Sugar Act, the Tea Act, and the Intolerable Acts. Have them create a protest sign that they might have carried to the rally. Signs should explain the reasons for the protest. **[Block Scheduling]**

★ ★

TEAM TEACHING STRATEGIES

The French and Indian War

GOAL

In this activity, students will learn about the French and Indian War by creating materials for a television documentary about Robert Rogers, an American soldier who fought in the war.

PLANNING

- **Purpose** This activity may be used in combination with teacher-directed lessons, as an enrichment activity, or as a performance-based assessment of content mastery.

- **Suggested Time** Plan to spend two lesson blocks and one homework assignment on this activity. Provide time for students to show and discuss the materials for their documentaries.

- **Teaching Team** At least one social studies teacher and one language arts teacher should take part in teaching this activity.

- **Group Size** This activity works best as a group activity. Groups should consist of three to five students. This activity might also be assigned as an extra credit option for individual students.

- **Materials and Resources** Provide students with copies of *The Impossible Major Rogers* by Patricia Lee Gauch and Rubric 22: Multimedia Presentations in the *Alternative Assessment Handbook*. Have students use their textbooks and other resources to help them gather information about Robert Rogers and the French and Indian War.

IMPLEMENTATION

1. Give students an overview of the activity by explaining that they will first study the book *The Impossible Major Rogers* by Patricia Lee Gauch. They will then create scripts and other related materials for a television documentary on Robert Rogers, an American military leader who took part in the French and Indian War.

2. Using the information under the heading "The French and Indian War" in Section 1 of the chapter as a guide, lead students in a discussion of this conflict. Then mention that *The Impossible Major Rogers* tells of the exploits of Major Robert Rogers, who led a group of American frontier fighters in the French and Indian War.

3. Next, have students read *The Impossible Major Rogers*. As they read, have students consider and note answers to the following questions: What was Rogers's background, and how did it prepare him for life as a frontier fighter? What military tactics did Rogers employ? What were Rogers's opinions of the French? What were his opinions of the Native Americans allied with the French? Of the Native Americans allied with the British? In what battles did Rogers take part? Which do you think was the most important battle? Why? How important do you think Rogers's exploits were to a British victory in the French and Indian War?

4. When students have completed their reading, tell them that their task is to develop a script and other related materials for a documentary on the role that Robert Rogers played in the French and Indian War. Inform students that the materials for their documentaries should be based on the notes they made during their reading of *The Impossible Major Rogers* and on any research they conducted on Rogers's life and his exploits. Mention that the documentary materials should include a title; an annotated list of the major topics to be covered; a script; sample visual materials, such as pictures and maps; and storyboards for re-enactments of incidents in Rogers's life. Remind students that the script should not only tell the "story" of the documentary but also link the various visuals and re-enactments together. Suggest that students review Rubric 22, which lists the basic requirements for preparing multimedia presentations, before they begin developing their documentary materials. If video equipment is available, encourage students to film sample scenes from their scripts.

5. Conclude by having groups show their sample scenes or display their documentary materials for the rest of the class. Group members should explain their scenes or materials and answer any questions from the class.

ASSESSMENT

1. To assess students' documentaries, use Rubric 22: Multimedia Presentations in the *Alternative Assessment Handbook* or in a customizable format on the One-Stop Planner.

2. Additional grades can be based on students' participation in the presentation and discussion of the documentary materials.

BLOCK SCHEDULING LESSON PLANS

THINK ABOUT THEMES

Citizenship

Agree Citizens should be responsible for determining how their government is run.

Disagree Citizens have an obligation to obey the government.

Constitutional Heritage

Agree Slavery violated natural rights and therefore should be abolished.

Disagree Slavery was a necessary evil because of the needs of society.

Global Relations

Agree Nations that have a wealth of resources can easily defeat less resouceful countries.

Disagree Weaker countries can use decisive planning and strategies to defeat a nation with more resources.

LESSON 1

(For use with Sections 1 and 2, pp. 184–93)

OBJECTIVES

1. Describe the actions taken by the First Continental Congress.

2. Evaluate how the fighting at Lexington and Concord affected the colonies' dispute with Great Britain.

3. Analyze the accomplishments of the Second Continental Congress.

4. Explain the ways that geography influenced the early battles of the war.

5. Evaluate the influence of Thomas Paine's *Common Sense* on the colonies.

6. Identify the main ideas stated in the Declaration of Independence, and explain Americans' reaction to it.

LET'S GET STARTED!

Have students imagine a situation in which people are unhappy with their system of government or with their political leaders. Ask them to decide what circumstances would make it appropriate for people to overthrow a government and create a new one. Also, have them consider what difficulties people might consider when deciding whether to join a revolutionary movement. Record students' responses on a sheet of butcher paper and retain it for later reference. Encourage them to think about these points as they study Sections 1 and 2.

TEACH OBJECTIVE 1

All Levels: Tell students to imagine that they are members of the First Continental Congress. Have them elect a secretary for the group. Then ask them to discuss how to respond to the crisis in Boston, and have the secretary take notes. After the discussion, ask the secretary to read back the notes. Tell students to use these ideas to assemble their own list of 10 resolutions. **[English Language Learners]**

TEACH OBJECTIVE 2

Levels 2 and 3: Organize students into small groups. Assign half the groups to read "The Shot Heard Round the World," and the other half to read "Paul Revere's Ride," both by Henry Wadsworth Longfellow. Direct groups to analyze the poem to determine how the fighting at Lexington and Concord affected the colonists' conflicts with Britain. **[Cooperative Learning]**

TEACH OBJECTIVE 3

Level 1: Ask students to tell you the accomplishments of the Second Continental Congress. List students' responses on the chalkboard. Then ask each student to choose which accomplishment they think is the most important. Ask each student to write a short paragraph explaining his or her answer. Encourage volunteers to share their paragraphs with the class. **[English Language Learners]**

TEACH OBJECTIVE 4

All Levels: Give students two blank maps: one of the Boston area and one of northern New York, in 1776. Have students illustrate their maps to show how geography influenced the early battles of the war. **[English Language Learners]**

TEACH OBJECTIVE 5

All Levels: Organize students into groups. Tell groups to imagine that they are colonists reading *Common Sense* in 1776. Have each group write a pamphlet explaining the colonists' response to Paine's work and the influence of *Common Sense* on the colonies. **[English Language Learners, Cooperative Learning]**

TEACH OBJECTIVE 6

All Levels: Organize the class into small groups. Have each group use the textbook to gather information about the main ideas in the Declaration of Independence and Americans' reactions to it. Have them use this information to add a chapter to the textbook. Tell students that their chapters should be at least two pages long, contain both primary and secondary quotations, and include appropriate images. **[English Language Learners, Cooperative Learning]**

REVIEW AND ASSESS

Have students complete the **Sections 1** and **2 Review** questions. Then assign students the roles

of different people who lived in the 1770s, including African Americans, American Indians, farmers, men, shopkeepers, and women. Have them write a newspaper editorial from one of these perspectives discussing what the phrase "all men are created equal" meant for them. Then have students complete **Daily Quiz 7.1** and **7.2.**

RETEACH

Have students complete **Main Idea Activities for English Language Learners and Special-Needs Students 7.1** and **7.2.** Then write each lesson objective on a separate sheet of butcher paper. Organize students into six groups and provide each group with one of the sheets of butcher paper. Have each group create and present a visual that they think best answers the lesson objective. **[English Language Learners, Cooperative Learning]**

EXTEND

Display the list of responses recorded during the Let's Get Started! activity. Ask students to consider this list and information from the lesson to decide whether the colonists were justified in declaring their independence. **[Block Scheduling]**

LESSON 2

(For use with Section 3, pp. 198–201)

OBJECTIVES

1. Examine the Patriots' advantages and disadvantages at the beginning of the Revolutionary War.

2. Explore the contributions that various groups made to the war effort.

3. Describe the problems the Patriots faced in Canada and New York.

LET'S GET STARTED!

Ask students if any of them have played on a sports team that defeated an opponent even though it seemed as if that opponent had all of the advantages. Then tell students that at the beginning of the Revolutionary War, it seemed that Great Britain had a huge advantage over the colonies.

TEACH OBJECTIVE 1

Level 1: Write the following phrases on the chalkboard: *military power, availability of resources, public support, dedication to the cause.* Have volunteers come to the chalkboard to take notes on how well each side was prepared in each of these areas. Then read the text under the heading "Comparing Strengths and Weaknesses" on pages 198–99 aloud, while volunteers take notes under the appropriate headings. After the section has been read and the notes have been completed, lead a discussion on which side students would expect to prevail. **[English Language Learners]**

TEACH OBJECTIVE 2

Level 2. Have students review the text to learn about the contributions made by African Americans, American Indians, and women in the Revolutionary War. Then have students create a resumé for one of these persons.

TEACH OBJECTIVE 3

All Levels: Organize the class into small groups. Then have groups use their textbooks or to write a 10-minute lesson on fighting in Canada and New York. Direct students to focus on the strategies employed by the two sides, the outcome of the battle, and the battle's significance. **[English Language Learners, Cooperative Learning]**

REVIEW AND ASSESS

Have students complete the **Section 3** and **4 Review** questions. Then have students prepare a table of contents for a magazine about the Revolutionary War. Have students select events and persons discussed in Section 3 to be the subjects of feature articles. They should then create titles for these articles and a synopsis. Then have students complete **Daily Quiz 7.3** and **7.4.**

RETEACH

Have students complete **Main Idea Activities for English Language Learners and Special-Needs Students 7.3.** Then have students write the section's headings and subheadings on a sheet of paper. Ask them to describe the main ideas under each heading and subheading. Have students compare and correct their outlines. **[English Language Learners]**

EXTEND

Ask students to think about how the war looked for the Patriots after the early battles in Canada and New York. Have students write a short paper predicting the outcome of the war, based only on the information in Sections 1 through 3 of Chapter 7. **[Block Scheduling]**

LESSON 3

(For use with Sections 4 and 5, pp. 202–13)

OBJECTIVES

1. Analyze George Washington's strategies at Trenton and Princeton.

2. Discuss the Battle of Saratoga as a turning point in the war.

3. Identify how foreign nations and individuals aided the Patriots.

4. Describe how the Patriots carried out the naval war.

5. Explain how geography affected the Patriot strategy in the West and how the war took place in the southern colonies.

6. Examine the events that finally ended the fighting.

LET'S GET STARTED!

Ask students to consider the following question: What relevance does the American Revolution have for us today? Prompt discussion by encouraging students to consider the political principles for which the American Revolution was fought.

TEACH OBJECTIVE 1

Level 1: Draw a compare-and-contrast chart on the chalkboard. On the vertical axis, write the headings: *Battle of Trenton, Battle of Princeton.* On the horizontal axis, write the headings: *Location, Leaders and Troops Involved, War Strategies.* As a class, fill in the chart. **[English Language Learners]**

TEACH OBJECTIVE 2

All Levels: Have students work in groups to develop a "You Are There" television program on the Battle of Saratoga. One group member should act as a narrator/interviewer who tells the story of the battle and interviews various people for their opinions. Other group members should play the following roles: an American soldier, a British officer, a British political leader, an American political leader, an American bystander, and a foreign observer. Have groups "broadcast" their programs. **[Cooperative Learning]**

TEACH OBJECTIVE 3

Level 3: Organize the class into two groups. In a formal debate, have one group support the following statement and have the other group oppose it. RESOLVED: "That the colonies could not have won their independence without French aid." Tell students to develop a written argument by using information from their textbooks. When students have prepared, stage a controlled debate in which as many students as possible get to make a statement for his or her group. **[Cooperative Learning]**

TEACH OBJECTIVE 4

Level 1: Have students create a series of storyboards that show how the Patriots fought the naval war. Remind students that storyboards tell a story using pictures only. Display completed storyboards around the classroom. **[English Language Learners]**

TEACH OBJECTIVE 5

Level 2: Organize students into pairs to develop a dialogue that might have taken place between George Rogers Clark and Francis Marion. Suggest that they include such topics as the types of people Clark and Marion recruited, their military tactics, how geography influenced these tactics, their triumphs and defeats, and their contribution to the American victory in the Revolutionary War. **[Cooperative Learning]**

TEACH OBJECTIVE 6

Level 2: Have students write a short press release announcing the end of the Revolutionary War. Press releases should include information about the Battle of Yorktown and outline the terms of the Treaty of Paris.

REVIEW AND ASSESS

Have students complete the **Sections 4** and **5 Review** questions. Then have each student select five items to place in a time capsule covering the last years of the Revolutionary War. Call on volunteers to list and explain the historical significance of their selected items. Finally, have students complete **Daily Quiz 7.4** and **7.5.**

RETEACH

Have students complete **Main Idea Activities for English Language Learners and Special-Needs Students 7.4** and **7.5.** Then have students prepare a chart headed *American Goals in the Revolutionary War*. On the left side of the chart have students list the dates *1775* and *1781*. Ask students to skim the chapter and fill in American goals in 1775 and in 1781. **[English Language Learners]**

EXTEND

Tell students that the majority of American Indians who took up arms fought with the British. Organize students into groups of four and have group members role-play American Indians—two who sided with the British and two who sided with the colonists. Ask groups to write a converstaion that might have taken place among American Indians about the wisdom of becoming involved in the conflict. **[Block Scheduling, Cooperative Learning]**

TEAM TEACHING STRATEGIES

Choosing Sides

GOAL

In this activity, students will learn how the American Revolution divided families and friends by writing letters explaining the Loyalist or Patriot point of view.

PLANNING

- **Purpose**   This activity may be used in combination with teacher-directed lessons, as an enrichment activity, or as a performance-based assessment of content mastery.

- **Suggested Time**   Plan to spend two lesson blocks and two homework assignments on this activity. Provide time for students to present and discuss their letters.

- **Teaching Team**   At least one social studies teacher and one language arts teacher should take part in teaching this activity.

- **Group Size**   Students should work in pairs, with one partner taking the role of Sam Meeker and the other taking the role of Mr. Meeker.

- **Materials and Resources**   Provide students with copies of the novel *My Brother Sam is Dead* by James Collier. In addition, you might distribute copies of Rubric 25: Personal Letters in the *Alternative Assessment Handbook*. Have students use their textbooks to help them learn more about the split between the Loyalists and the Patriots.

IMPLEMENTATION

1. Give students an overview of the activity by explaining that they will first study the novel *My Brother Sam Is Dead* by James Lincoln Collier and Christopher Collier. Then they will write letters that two characters in the novel might have written.

2. Lead students in a discussion of the conflicts and divided loyalties that the American Revolution created among family members and between friends. Encourage students to conduct research on the Loyalists and the Patriots. Suggest that they look for answers to the following questions. Who were they? What were their backgrounds? In which areas did many Loyalists and Patriots live? What were their views on the American Revolution? Next, mention that the novel that students will read, *My Brother Sam Is Dead*, is the story of Tim Meeker, Tim's family is split by the American Revolution when his brother Sam joins the Patriot cause, but his father remains loyal to Great Britain.

3. Have students read the novel. As they read, have students note answers to the following questions: What is the book about? Who are the major characters in the story? What are Sam's reasons for joining the Patriots? Why does Mr. Meeker choose to remain loyal to Great Britain? How does Tim view the split in his family?

4. When students have completed their reading, tell pairs that their task is to write letters that might have been written by Sam Meeker and Mr. Meeker. One member of the pair should write a letter from Sam to his father explaining why he became a Patriot and

why the rest of the family should join the cause. The other member of the pair should write a letter from Mr. Meeker to Sam explaining why he remained loyal to Britain and why Sam should abandon the Patriots. Inform students that their letters should be based on the notes they made during their reading of the novel and on their research on Loyalists and Patriots. Before they begin this task, have students review the Rubric 25: Personal Letters.

5. Conclude by calling on pairs to volunteer to read their letters to the class. Then lead discussion about steps they might take to reconcile family members whose divided loyalties set them against one another.

ASSESSMENT

1. To assess students' letters, use the Rubric 25: Personal Letters in the *Alternative Assessment Handbook* or in a customizable format on the One-Stop Planner.

2. Additional grades can be based on students' participation in the concluding discussion.

Forming a Government

★ ★

BLOCK SCHEDULING LESSON PLANS

THINK ABOUT THEMES

Global Relations

Agree New nations are not strong.

Disagree A country's strength is not determined by its age.

Citizenship

Agree People have certain rights that should never be taken away.

Disagree The government should be able to choose which rights citizens have.

Constitutional Heritage

Agree A state government should be stronger than the federal government.

Disagree A strong federal government creates a more powerful country.

LESSON 1

(For use with Sections 1 and 2, pp. 222–35)

OBJECTIVES

1. Describe the ideas and documents that shaped American belief about governments, and evaluate how state constitutions contributed to the development of representative government.

2. List the powers held by the central government under the Articles of Confederation.

3. Explain what the Nortwest Ordinance accomplished.

4. Describe how other nations treated the new U.S. government.

5. Examine the economic problems that arose under the Articles of Confederation.

6. Analyze the causes and consequences of Shays's Rebellion.

LET'S GET STARTED!

Ask students to name some of the causes of the Revolutionary War. *(Students' responses might be objections to unfair taxes, a lack of representation in government, or a desire for greater personal freedom.)*

Ask students why they think opposition to taxation would make the former colonists fearful of a strong central government. *(Students' responses might be that taxes were levied by a strong central government in Great Britain.)* Tell students that the desire to be represented fairly and equally in the lawmaking process was probably the most important issue for the colonists.

TEACH OBJECTIVE 1

Level 1: Ask students to discuss the different ideas and documents that influenced American ideas of representative government. List students' responses on the chalkboard. Then divide the class into small groups and assign each topic to a group. Have groups write a paragraph explaining how important their topic was to the development of American government. After groups have completed their paragraphs, have them present their explanations to the class. **[English Language Learners, Cooperative Learning]**

All Levels: Organize the class into small groups, and have group members imagine that they are editors who have been assigned to determine the contents of a special edition of a newsmagazine. Inform groups that their magazines should cover the time period from 1777 to 1787. Ask groups to produce headlines and write brief summaries for several articles about the influences on the development of representative democracy, including ideas, documents, and state constitutions. Direct groups to write each headline and summary on a separate sheet of butcher paper or posterboard. You may also wish to direct groups to create or find an illustration or map to accompany their headline and summary. **[English Language Learners, Cooperative Learning]**

TEACH OBJECTIVE 2

Level 1: Have students make a series of postcards illustrating a power of the federal government as articulated in the Articles of Confederation. **[English Language Learners]**

TEACH OBJECTIVE 3

All Levels: Have students work in small groups to create a brochure about advantages of moving to the Northwest Territory following passage of the Land Ordinance of 1785 and the Northwest Ordinance of 1787. Tell students to explain in their brochure how the Northwest Ordinance improved life for Americans in this region and how the territory will join the United States as states. Encourage students to include testimonials from citizens who have already moved to the Northwest Territory. **[English Language Learners, Cooperative Learning]**

TEACH OBJECTIVE 4

Level 1: Ask students to think about some of the economic problems that arose under the Articles of Confederation. Then have students make a poster that illustrates one of these problems. Encourage volunteers to share their posters to the class. **[English Language Learners]**

TEACH OBJECTIVE 5

Level 1: Organize students into small groups. Assign each group the role of officials representing either the British or Spanish governments. Ask each group to write a short report to send to the leaders of its respective country with recommendations on how it ought to treat the U.S. government. Remind students that the Articles of Confederation made the U.S. national govern-

ment weak. **[English Language Learners, Cooperative Learning]**

TEACH OBJECTIVE 6

Level 1: Ask students to create a set of "before" and "after" pictures. "Before" pictures should show the problems that led to Shays's Rebellion. "After" pictures should show how Shays's Rebellion affected Americans' perception of the national government. **[English Language Learners]**

Level 2: Ask students to create a political cartoon describing the causes and consequences of Shays's Rebellion. Have students include a caption that explains their cartoon.

REVIEW AND ASSESS

Have students complete the **Sections 1** and **2 Review** questions. Then ask students to write a paragraph to support or oppose continuing the government of the United States under the Articles of Confederation. Tell students that in forming their opinions they should consider the powers given to and denied the central government and the international and economic problems that the central government faced. Have students with opposing views read their paragraphs to the class. Then have students complete **Daily Quiz 8.1** and **8.2**.

RETEACH

Have students complete **Main Idea Activities for English Language Learners and Special-Needs Students 8.1** and **8.2**. Draw students' attention to the British magazine's characterization of the new nation as the "Dis-United States." Have students work in small groups to create a two-column chart. Instruct them to label one column *United States* and the other *Dis-United States*. Under the first heading, have them list examples from the lesson that show that the states were united. Tell students to list under the second heading examples that show that the states were disunited. Call on volunteers to present their charts to the class. Use the charts as a starting point for a class discussion about the relative unity or disunity of the states in the mid-1780s. **[English Language Learners]**

EXTEND

Encourage students to read the novel *The Winter Hero* by James Lincoln Collier and Christopher Collier, which tells the story of Shays's Rebellion from the viewpoint of a young man named Justin Conkey. Ask students to write a brief speech that Justin might have made explaining to the Massachusetts government officials what caused the rebellion, what he did to help Shays's cause, and the consequences of the rebellion. **[Block Scheduling]**

LESSON 2

(For use with Sections 3 and 4, pp. 236–47)

OBJECTIVES

1. Explain why delegates met for the Constitutional Convention, and examine the main issues debated and compromises reached there.

2. Describe how the federal government is balanced under the U.S. Constitution.

3. Explain why some people were against the new Constitution, and examine the *Federalist Papers'* arguments for the Constitution.

4. Describe when and how the Constitution was ratified, and identify the reasons some people wanted a bill of rights, and explain how it was added to the Constitution.

LET'S GET STARTED!

Write the word *compromise* on the chalkboard. Call on volunteers to offer a definition of the word, noting their responses on the chalkboard. Then tell students that in this lesson they will learn that through a series of compromises, representatives of the "disunited" states were able to design a new framework of government—the Constitution.

TEACH OBJECTIVE 1

Level 1: Write the names of the following people or groups of people in a column on the chalkboard: *James Madison, William Paterson, Edmund Randolph, all delegates,* and *southern delegates.*

Write the following terms in another column: *Virginia Plan, New Jersey Plan, Great Compromise,* and *Three-Fifths Compromise.* Have students match the person or group with the ideas that the person or group advanced or supported at the Constitutional Convention. Remind students that some ideas will have more than one supporter. After students have completed matching names and ideas, ask volunteers to provide a definition for each term. **[English Language Learners]**

Level 2: Have students create an annotated flow chart of the important events that led to delegates meeting at the Constitutional Convention. In addition, have students use their flowcharts to examine the issues debated and the compromises reached there.

TEACH OBJECTIVE 2

Level 1: Organize students into two groups. Have students in one group each draw a diagram illustrating how the system of checks and balances works. Have students in the other group each draw a diagram illustrating how the federal system works. Have volunteers present their groups' diagrams to the class. **[English Language Learners, Cooperative Learning]**

TEACH OBJECTIVE 3

Level 1: Remind students that the Antifederalists and the Federalist had very different ideas about the new Constitution. Write the following phrases on the chalkboard: *central government, individual rights, new government.* Ask students to explain how the Antifederalists and the Federalists differed on each of these issues with regard to Constitution. **[English Language Learners]**

Level 2: Have students read *Federalist Paper* "No. 10." Then have them create a book jacket for this essay. Jacket blurbs should summarize the *Federalist Papers'* arguments for supporting the constitution. Tell students that the book jackets should be catchy and give viewers a reason to read and buy the essay.

TEACH OBJECTIVE 4

Level 1: Organize the class so that each student has a partner. Give each pair a blank outline map of the original 13 states. Tell students to label each state, as well as the date that it formally ratified the Constitution. **[English Language Learners, Cooperative Learning]**

Level 3: Ask students to imagine that they are members of Congress who support adding a bill of rights to the Constitution. Then have each student write a speech to deliver to Congress to persuade other representatives. Ask volunteers to share their speeches with the class.

REVIEW AND ASSESS

Have students complete the **Sections 3** and **4 Review** questions. Organize students into small groups. Tell each group to identify what they think are the 10 most important events in Sections 3 and 4. Then have each group create an annotated time line of these events. In each annotation, have students identify the significance of the event in relation to the establishment of the new government. Then have students complete **Daily Quiz 8.3** and **8.4.**

RETEACH

Have students complete the **Main Idea Activities for English Language Learners and Special-Needs Students 8.3** and **8.4.** Then ask students to work in pairs to create a glossary that would accompany a new textbook on the drafting and ratification of the Constitution. Tell students that the glossary should include key terms, notable individuals, major plans, and significant compromises discussed in the lesson. Call on pairs to share their work with the rest of the class. **[English Language Learners]**

EXTEND

Remind students that African Americans, American Indians, and women did not participate in the Constitutional Convention. Then ask students to write letters to the editor commenting on the various terms of the Constitution from the viewpoint of an African American, an American Indian, or a woman. Encourage students to share and compare their letters. **[Block Scheduling]**

Forming a Government

★ ★

TEAM TEACHING STRATEGIES

The U.S. Government

GOAL

In this activity, students will learn about how the new nation developed a governmental system by creating slogans and banners that describe and illustrate the special qualities of American government.

PLANNING

- **Purpose** This activity may be used in combination with teacher-directed lessons, as an enrichment activity, or as a performance-based assessment of content mastery.

- **Suggested Time** Plan to spend one lesson block and one homework assignment on this activity. Provide time for students to display and discuss their slogans and banners.

- **Teaching Team** At least one social studies teacher and one language arts teacher should take part in teaching this activity.

- **Group Size** Have students work in groups of three or four. To ensure that all students are fully involved in the activity, you might suggest that each group member take primary responsibility for particular tasks.

- **Materials and Resources** Provide students with copies of *A View of America*. You might also provide students with copies of Rubric 34: Slogans and Banners in the *Alternative Assessment Handbook*. Have students use their textbooks and other resources to help them gather information about the nature of U.S. government.

IMPLEMENTATION

1. Give students an overview of this activity by explaining that they will learn more about the United States's new system of government by first reading an excerpt from a letter, written by Michel-Guillaume-Jean de Crèvecoeur, that describes the unique character of American society. Then they will create slogans and banners that describe and illustrate the special qualities of American government.

2. Ask students to skim Sections 1, 3, and 4 of the chapter. Then lead students in a discussion of the unique qualities and special nature of the American governmental system. Focus attention on how this system of government compared with European governments of the time. Provide students with pointers by mentioning such key words and phrases as *democracy, federalism, checks and balances*, and *individual rights*.

3. Distribute copies of the excerpt from Crèvecoeur's letter and the rubric to students. Provide students with the following biographical information on the author: Crèvecoeur was born in France and originally came to North America to fight for the French in the French and Indian War. In the late 1760s he settled on a farm in New York. There, he adopted the name J. Hector St. John and wrote the series of essays that became known as *Letters from an American Farmer*. He served as French envoy to the United States from 1783 to 1790, when he returned to France.

Continue by working through the excerpt with students, asking them to consider the following as they read: What differences does Crèvecoeur see between American society and European society? According to Crèvecoeur, what special qualities do American citizens possess? What transforms people from "invisible" Europeans to American citizens? Encourage students to take notes as they read.

4. Tell groups to select what they think are the five most important or striking features of American government. Then they will design slogans and banners that describe and illustrate these features. Have students base their slogans and banners on notes taken during class discussions as well as on the reading of the Crèvecoeur excerpt and any research on American government that they have undertaken. Point out that slogans might make comparisons between the United States and Europe, offering the following as an example: *Europe: Where Monarchs Rule. United States: Where the People Rule.* Encourage groups to decorate their banners with symbols or other appropriate illustrations.

5. Have groups display their banners around the classroom. Conclude by calling on group members to discuss their slogans and explain why they selected specific features as the most important or striking. Encourage other members of the class to ask questions.

ASSESSMENT

1. To assess students' slogans and banners, use the Rubric 34: Slogans and Banners in the *Alternative Assessment Handbook* or in a customizable format on the One-Stop Planner.

2. Additional grades can be based on students' participation in the concluding discussion.

★ ★

BLOCK SCHEDULING LESSON PLANS

THINK ABOUT THEMES

Constitutional Heritage

Agree A country's leader with too much power will become a dictator.

Disagree The leader of a country must have a great deal of power in order to run the government.

Citizenship

Agree One vote cast out of millions of votes cannot affect a presidential election.

Disagree Past elections have shown that every American's vote counts.

Culture

Agree The rights of any group are more important than the interests of all people.

Disagree The rights and interests of all Americans should be regarded equally.

LESSON 1

(For use with Sections 1 and 2, pp. 256–61; 284–89)

OBJECTIVES

1. Explain how the framers of the Constitution tried to balance state and federal powers.

2. List the three branches of the federal government, describe the requirements for membership in each branch, and analyze the division of power among them.

3. Discuss the main freedoms outlined by the First Amendment, and analyze why they are important.

4. Outline how the Bill of Rights addresses colonial grievances listed in the Declaration of Independence, and examine the protections that it gives to people accused of crimes.

LET'S GET STARTED!

Ask students to consider what would happen if the U.S. government had little authority over the people. *(Students's responses might suggest ideas such as a rise in crime, a lack of participation in the nation's armed forces, or a lack of money to run government programs.)* Explain to students that the U.S. government under the Articles of Confederation had many weaknesses. Then ask students to describe what can happen when a government has too much authority. *(Students's responses might be that an overly powerful government might violate its citizens' rights or attack other countries.)* Tell students that in this lesson they will learn about the U.S. Constitution. Explain that the Constitution was designed to correct the weaknesses of the Articles of Confederation while still protecting people's rights.

TEACH OBJECTIVE 1

Level 1: Write the following powers on the chalkboard: *declaring war, regulating trade between states and with foreign countries, taxing, establishing local governments, providing for the nation's defense, conducting elections, enforcing laws, regulating education, providing for citizens' welfare, coining money, conducting diplomacy, regulating trade within each state, borrowing money.* Tell students that these are examples of delegated, reserved, and concurrent powers. Review definitions of these words with students. Then ask students to identify whether each of the powers that are listed on the board are held by the federal government, state governments, or are shared. **[English Language Learners]**

Level 3: Tell students to imagine that they need to explain the balance of national and state powers to a person from another country. Ask students to write a report explaining the federal system. Tell students to give examples of concurrent, delegated, and reserved powers in their reports.

TEACH OBJECTIVE 2

Level 2: Tell students that they have been assigned to describe the U.S. government to citizens of another country who are considering changing their nation's form of government. Have students work in small groups to write a memorandum that describes the three branches of the federal government and the requirements for membership in each. Memos should also analyze the division of power. After groups have finished, have each group explain its memorandum to the country seeking the information (the class). **[Cooperative Learning]**

Level 3: Have students write a letter to an Antifederalist, explaining to him or her whether they think the three branches of government share power equally. If not, which branch do they think has the most power? Have students explain their answers.

TEACH OBJECTIVE 3

Level 1: Tell students that they have been assigned to describe the U.S. government to officials of another country who are considering changing their form of government. Have students work in small groups to create a poster showing one of the freedoms protected by the First Amendment. Tell students that both posters should rely on the use of images rather than words. Upon completion of the activity, have each group display and explain its posters to the class. **[English Language Learners, Cooperative Learning]**

All Levels: Have students work in small groups to create advertisements for a law firm that specializes in protecting one of the rights listed in the First Amendment. Advertisements may be designed for print, radio, or television depending on available resources. Advertisements should focus on scenarios in which the First Amendment rights of citizens appear to have been violated.

Once groups have finished, have them present their advertisements to the class. After each presentation, have the class discuss the situation illustrated and identify which freedom has been violated. **[English Language Learners, Cooperative Learning]**

TEACH OBJECTIVE 4

Level 1: Create a two-column chart on the chalkboard that lists the words, *Fifth Amendment, Sixth Amendment,* up through *Tenth Amendment.* In the second column, write a brief description of each amendment. Ask volunteers to read these descriptions aloud. Organize students into six groups. Assign each group one of these amendments. Have each group create a poster that illustrates what rights are protected by its assigned amendment. After groups have completed their posters, ask them to share their work with the class. **[English Language Learners]**

Level 3: Ask volunteers to read aloud the Third and Fourth Amendments. Then have students write a short story that explains why the issues raised by the amendment were important to the writers of the Bill of Rights.

REVIEW AND ASSESS

Have students complete the **Sections 1** and **2 Review** questions. Then organize students into small groups and provide each group with a set of eight index cards. Have students label the first seven cards *Article I* through *Article VII,* and the eighth card *Bill of Rights.* Have groups write on the back of each card a brief summary of what each article or the Bill of Rights addresses. Have groups share their cards with the class. Then have students complete **Daily Quiz 9.1** and **9.2.**

RETEACH

Have students complete **Main Idea Activities for English Language Learners and Special-Needs Students 9.1** and **9.2.** Then have students work in small groups to create a study guide for this lesson. Study guides might contain true/false questions, short answers, and fill-in-the blank sentences. Have each group exchange its guide with another group. Group members should then work together to answer the questions included in the study guide. **[English Language Learners]**

EXTEND

Organize the class into several small groups and have each group develop a Class Constitution for running the classroom. Students must decide how they will divide the powers among the teacher, the principal, and the students. They must also decide on a list of rights they would like to include in a Class Bill of Rights. Remind students that the document must clearly protect students' rights while focusing on creating an effective classroom. Have groups present their constitution and class bill of rights to the class. **[Cooperative Learning, Block Scheduling]**

LESSON 2

(For use with Section 3, pp. 290–95)

OBJECTIVES

1. Describe how a person can become a U.S. citizen.

2. Identify some of the most important responsibilities of citizenship.

3. Evaluate why citizens should be involved with their community and government.

LET'S GET STARTED!

Ask the class what it means to be a U.S. citizen. *(Students' responses might be that U.S. citizens have certain rights that are not necessarily protected in other countries.)* List their responses on the chalkboard. Explain to students that there is no correct answer but that many people associate U.S. citizenship with certain rights. Then tell students that in addition to the rights U.S. citizens enjoy, there are responsibilities that U.S. citizens should observe. Tell students that in this lesson they will learn about U.S. citizenship.

TEACH OBJECTIVE 1

Level 1: Remind students that almost all children born in the United States as well as almost all children born in U.S. territories automatically become U.S. citizens even if their parents are not citizens. Have the class make a large world map and highlight the United States and its territories to show these areas. If there are students in the class who were born in other countries, have them place a thumbtack on the country in which they were born. **[English Language Learners]**

Level 3: Tell students to imagine they are a lawmaker, and a group of other lawmakers wants to change the naturalization process. Have students review information on the process. Then have students use this information to write an editorial in which they defend this process to their fellow lawmakers.

TEACH OBJECTIVE 2

All Levels: Tell students that during the naturalization process, immigrants must take a test to prove that they have a basic understanding of U.S. history and government. Provide students with an example of this test. (Most books on citizenship have sample tests.) Then have students develop a 25-question test on the rights and responsibilities of U.S. citizens. Suggest that students frame their questions in a fashion similar to those in the sample tests. Pair students, and have partners exchange and complete each other's tests. **[English Language Learners, Cooperative Learning]**

Level 3: Have students examine newspapers and magazines from recent months to find information on an elected official or a recent trial. Then have students use this information to create a campaign poster that encourages people to vote—for their candidate in particular—or to create a poster highlighting the importance of serving on a jury.

TEACH OBJECTIVE 3

Level 1: Review the differences between rights and responsibilities with the class. Then create a three-column chart on the chalkboard. In the first column, randomly list the rights and responsibilities of U.S. citizens. Label the second column *Rights* and the third column *Responsibilities*. For each right or responsibility listed in the first column, have students identify which category it falls under and place a check mark in the appropriate column. Ask students to explain why they classified each item as they did. **[English Language Learners]**

Level 3: Review with students different ways that citizens can be involved with their community and government that are listed in the textbook. Then ask students to brainstorm their own list of ways that citizens can be involved. Next to each item on their list, students should explain how it would benefit the community.

REVIEW AND ASSESS

Have students complete the **Section 3 Review** questions. Then have students create a collage depicting people who are actively taking part in their community or government. Discuss the importance of citizen involvement in a representative democracy and review the responsibilities that are part of being a U.S. citizen. Then have students complete **Daily Quiz 9.3.**

RETEACH

Have students complete **Main Idea Activities for English Language Learners and Special-Needs Students 9.3.** Then ask them to take one key term from this section and write a few sentences detailing important information they learned about it. As a class, review each of the terms by having students read their descriptions. **[English Language Learners]**

EXTEND

Have the class discuss an issue that currently affects the community or the school. *(Students's responses might be issues as curbside recycling, underage drinking, school lunch menus, or school uniforms.)* Organize students into small groups, and assign each group a different issue. Then have groups write and circulate a petition that encourages others to support its position on this issue. **[Block Scheduling]**

TEAM TEACHING STRATEGIES

Good Citizens

GOAL

In this activity, students will learn about the rights and obligations of citizenship by writing a resumé for someone applying for the position of "good citizen."

PLANNING

- **Purpose** This activity may be used in combination with teacher-directed lessons, as an enrichment activity, or as a performance-based assessment of content mastery.

- **Suggested Time** Plan to spend one lesson block on this activity. Provide time for students to offer each other feedback on their finished resumés.

- **Teaching Team** At least one social studies teacher and one language arts teacher should take part in teaching this activity.

- **Group Size** This activity should be conducted as an individual assignment.

- **Materials and Resources** Provide students with copies of *The Free Citizen* by Theodore Roosevelt. You might also provide students with copies of the Rubric 31: Resumés in the *Alternative Assessment Handbook*. Have students use their textbooks to help them gather information about the rights and obligations of citizenship.

IMPLEMENTATION

1. Give students an overview of the activity by explaining that they will learn more about the rights and responsibilities of citizenship by writing a resumé for someone applying for the job of "good citizen."

2. Using Section 3 of the chapter as a guide, lead students in a discussion of the rights and responsibilities of citizens. Then distribute copies of the excerpt from Theodore Roosevelt's *The Free Citizen* and the rubric to students.

3. Introduce the excerpt by briefly identifying Roosevelt and informing students that they will learn more about him and his political philosophy later in the course. Continue by reading through the excerpt with students, asking them to consider the following as they read: What do you think Roosevelt considered the central feature of good citizenship? In Roosevelt's opinion, why is it important for Americans to make democracy succeed? What must people do in order to be entitled to full citizenship? What role does education play in effective citizenship? Encourage students to take notes as they discuss these questions.

4. Next, have students imagine they are applying for the position of "good citizen." Ask them to use the notes they made during class discussions and information in their textbooks to write a resumé to accompany an application for this position. Tell students that resumés should include biographical information (name, address, education, and so on), a brief description of the position they are applying for, a list of the major

characteristics of good citizenship, educational qualifications for citizenship (a course in civics or a lesson on the U.S. Constitution, for example), good citizenship activities they have participated in, and good citizenship activities they plan to undertake in the future. For further guidance, have students review Rubric 31: Resumés. Finally, have students write a short cover note explaining why they are seeking the position of "good citizen."

5. Conclude by asking volunteers to read their resumés and cover letters to the rest of the class. Have students use information gathered from these readings to write a sentence that summarizes the essence of good citizenship.

ASSESSMENT

1. To assess students' resumés, use the Rubric 31: Resumés in the *Alternative Assessment Handbook* or in a customizable format on the One-Stop Planner.

2. Additional grades can be based on students' summary sentences.

CHAPTER 10

Launching the Nation

★ ★

BLOCK SCHEDULING LESSON PLANS

THINK ABOUT THEMES

Global Relations

Agree A new country should focus only on domestic issues.

Disagree A new country should quickly establish itself as a global power.

Constitutional Heritage

Agree The framers scripted a document that continues to suit the needs of the country.

Disagree The language used in the document is open to interpretation.

Economics

Agree A country should strengthen its own economy before it satisfies foreign debts.

Disagree It is vital to international relations to maintain good financial standing with other countries.

LESSON 1

(For use with Sections 1 and 2, pp. 300–09)

OBJECTIVES

1. Explain why Americans elected George Washington as the first president, and identify their expectations of their new government.

2. Describe the steps Congress and the president took to organize the new government.

3. Identify the challenges Alexander Hamilton faced as Secretary of the Treasury and the issues his plans raised.

4. Describe the issues that Hamilton and Thomas Jefferson disagreed on, and explain their views.

5. Examine the questions that were raised when the Bank of the United States was founded, and examine the different views that Hamilton and Jeffereson had concerning the Bank.

LET'S GET STARTED!

Ask a volunteer to read the Preamble to the Constitution to the class. Have students write in their own words the goals listed in the Preamble. Then have students identify steps that they think the new government would need to take to accomplish these goals. Write students' responses on the chalkboard. Tell students that in this lesson they will learn more about the actions that President Washington, his cabinet, and Congress took to achieve these goals.

TEACH OBJECTIVE 1

Level 2: Have students draw a cartoon strip showing important events in the life of George Washington. Instruct students to include information about why Americans elected Washington and their expectations of him and the new government.

TEACH OBJECTIVE 2

Level 1: Write *Executive Branch* and *Judicial Branch* on the chalkboard. Remind students that the new government had to make important decisions regarding policies and procedures, including setting up the executive branch and the judicial branch. Ask students to copy the chart on a piece of paper, and then fill it in by explaining the steps that Congress and President Washington took to organize the national government. **[English Language Learners]**

Level 3: Draw students' attention to George Washington's quote under the "Setting Precedents" heading on page 303 in the textbook. Ask students to evaluate whether the first Congress and president accomplished their goal with regard to forming the judiciary.

TEACH OBJECTIVE 3

Level 2: Have students write entries for Alexander Hamilton's memoirs. Entries should describe his thoughts about the issues that faced the new government and his plans to meet these challenges. Entries should also mention the reactions of other people to his ideas.

TEACH OBJECTIVE 4

All Levels: Organize the class into pairs. Ask one member of each pair to take the role of Jefferson and the other member to take the role of Hamilton. Have pairs create dialogues demonstrating their differing views about the Constitution, government, the economy, and protective tariffs. Ask volunteers to perform their dialogues for the class. **[English Language Learners, Cooperative Learning]**

Level 3: Have students decide if Hamilton's or Jefferson's views about the Constitution, government, the economy, and protective tariffs more aptly reflect their own views. Ask students to write an essay explaining whose views they agree with and why.

TEACH OBJECTIVE 5

Level 1: Divide students in two groups. Tell one group they represent people who favor strict construction, and tell the other group they represent people who favor loose construction. Have each group work to create a paragraph explaining their point of view in the debate over the National Bank. **[English Language Learners, Cooperative Learning]**

All Levels: Tell students to imagine that they work for the Historical Broadcasting Network, the only radio station with a time machine. Their radio station is developing a documentary on the National Bank. Organize students into small groups. Remind students that a radio documentary usually consists of a narration on the major

topics interspersed with interviews with key individuals, experts, and "people in the street." Have groups use their textbooks and to find information on the debate and produce their radio documentary. **[English Language Learners, Cooperative Learning]**

REVIEW AND ASSESS

Have students complete the **Sections 1** and **2 Review** questions. Then assign each student a name, event, idea, trend, location, or development described in this section. Ask each student to prepare a mystery profile of his or her assigned topic that consists of a set of clues. Then organize students into pairs. Have students read their clues to their partners until they correctly identify the mystery topic. Then reverse roles. Have students take turns quizzing and being quizzed by various partners. Finally, have students complete **Daily Quiz 10.1** and **10.2.**

RETEACH

Have students complete **Main Idea Activities for English Language Learners and Special-Needs Students 10.1** and **10.2.** Then have students construct a three-column chart that lists the political, judicial, and economic problems the new government faced and the solutions that were found for these problems. **[English Language Learners]**

EXTEND

Have students use the library and other resources to research information about the presidential cabinet today. Then have students prepare press releases describing the function of each member of the cabinet. **[Block Scheduling]**

LESSON 2

(For use with Sections 3, 4, and 5, pp. 310–25)

OBJECTIVES

1. Explain how Americans responded to events in France, what President Washington's foreign policy was, and how the United States settled its disputes with Great Britain and Spain.

2. Identify the domestic problems faced by the United States.

3. Explain the advice that Washington gave the nation in his Farewell Address.

4. Explain how political parties formed and the role they played in the presidential election of 1796.

5. Describe the problems with foreign nations that John Adams faced as president as well as the Alien and Sedition Acts and the Republicans' response.

6. Analyze the main issues in the election of 1800 and some of the outcomes of the election.

LET'S GET STARTED!

Ask students whether they think a nation's foreign policy should be based on moral principle or self-interest. Then ask them how and why these two methods of determining foreign policy may conflict with each other. Inform students that in this lesson they will learn about conflicts between the United States and other nations in its early years. Also tell students that they will learn about several internal challenges that confronted the first U.S. presidents and governments.

TEACH OBJECTIVE 1

Level 1: Have students use the library to find additional information on the French Revolution. Then have students create a time line of the main events of the revolutionary period. Tell students that their time lines should include as many entries as are needed to summarize the revolutionary period. You may wish to have students annotate their time lines. **[English Language Learners]**

Level 1: Have students create three drawings. The first should depict the American response to events in France. The second should illustrate President Washington's foreign policy. The third should show how the United States settled its disputes with Great Britain and Spain. Ask volunteers to present their drawings to the class, and have students describe the story these drawings tell about the early years of the United States. **[English Language Learners]**

Level 3: Have students imagine that they are an American citizen living in the 1790s. Have students think about the signigicant events in the world around them, such as the French Revolution, President Washington's meeting with Edmond Genet, and treaties with Great Britain and Spain. Then have each student write a newspaper article describing these events.

TEACH OBJECTIVE 2

Level 2: Have students imagine that they are reporters at either the Battle of Fallen Timbers or the Whiskey Rebellion. Ask each student to write one interview question to ask members of each side in the dispute. Then have them supply a possible answer to that question. Questions and answers should illustrate why these events took place and how the U.S. government reacted to them.

TEACH OBJECTIVE 4

Level 1: Have students create a recruiting poster that might have been used by either the Federalist or Democratic-Republican parties prior to the 1796 election. Ask volunteers to present their posters to the class. Then have members of the class assume the roles of party members and respond to the poster's appeal. **[English Language Learners]**

Level 2: Have students review the text about Washington's Farewell Address on pages 317–318. Ask students to identify the key recommendations that Washington made regarding the U.S. government. Write these recommendations on the chalkboard. Then instruct students to write a sentence about each recommendation explaining whether they believe the United States should follow Washington's advice.

Level 3: Review with the class the advice that Washington gave to the nation about political parties in his Farewell Address. Than ask students how well the United States followed Washington's advice during the election of 1796. Have students write an addendum to the Farewell Address as if they were Washington. Ask students to cite examples from this section to support that assessment in the third column.

TEACH OBJECTIVE 5

Level 3: Have students write a newspaper editorial in which they evaluate President Adams's presidency. Students should consider how he handled such issues as the XYZ affair and the Alien and Sedition Acts.

TEACH OBJECTIVE 6

Level 1: Explain to students that the election of 1800 led to important changes to the presidential election process. Write the following statements on the chalkboard: *"Thomas Jefferson and Aaron Burr each win 73 electoral votes"* and *"In 1804 Congress passes the Twelfth Amendment."* Ask students to create a flow chart that uses these statements as the beginning and end. **[English Language Learners]**

Level 2: Organize the class into two groups. Have each group create a campaign pamphlet that includes quotations, pictures, drawings, and slogans for one of the two candidates in the 1800 presidential election.

REVIEW AND ASSESS

Have students complete the **Sections 3, 4,** and **5 Review** questions. Then organize the class into small groups. Have each group make up a list of the reasons President Washington opposed going to war against Great Britain. Ask them if Washington applied the same reasoning to going to war with the American Indian confederacy. Why might Washington see a difference between the two situations? When students have finished the activity, discuss their answers with the class. Then have students complete **Daily Quiz 10.3** and **10.4.**

RETEACH

Have students complete **Main Idea Activities for English Language Learners and Special-Needs Students 10.3, 10.4,** and **10.5.** Then organize the class into small groups. Ask each group to write down what its members consider to be the most important issue discussed in this lesson. Have each group prepare a list of questions about the issue that are answered in the text. Conclude by instructing each group to present its questions to the class and by having volunteers answer each question. **[English Language Learners]**

EXTEND

Organize the class into two groups: those who think Alexander Hamilton was a hero and those who think he was a villain. Then hold a debate between the two groups. Have each student prepare a one- or two-paragraph argument on their position before you begin the debate. **[Block Scheduling]**

★ ★

TEAM TEACHING STRATEGIES

John Adams—Biographical Maps

GOAL

In this activity, students will learn about the life of John Adams by constructing biographical maps.

PLANNING

- **Purpose** This activity may be used in combination with teacher-directed lessons, as an enrichment activity, or as a performance-based assessment of content mastery.

- **Suggested Time** Plan to spend two lesson blocks and one homework assignment on this activity. Provide time for students to display and discuss their biographical maps.

- **Teaching Team** At least one social studies teacher and one language arts teacher should take part in teaching this activity.

- **Group Size** Groups should consist of three to five students. However, you may choose to assign the activity as an extra credit option for individual students.

- **Materials and Resources** Provide groups with copies of the Rubric 20: Map Creation in the *Alternative Assessment Handbook*. You might also provide groups with sheets of butcher paper or posterboard. Have students use their textbooks to help them discover more about the life of John Adams. You will also need to provide students with copies of *John Adams: A Life* by John Ferling.

IMPLEMENTATION

1. Give students an overview of the activity by explaining that they will first study the book *John Adams: A Life* by John Ferling. They will then create two biographical maps. The first will show significant events in Adams's life up to and including the American Revolution. The second will show significant events in his life in the post-Revolution years.

2. Using the information in Section 5 of the chapter as a guide, lead students in a discussion of John Adams's tenure as president. Encourage students to note the significant events of Adams's presidency. Then mention that the book that students will read provides a full biographical study.

3. Next, have students read *John Adams: A Life*. As they read, have students consider and note what they think are the significant events and developments in Adams's life. Suggest that they make special note of the locations where these events and developments took place. Inform students that if they feel that the book does not provide sufficient details on a particular period in Adams's life, they should use library resources to locate this information.

4. When students have completed their reading, and tell groups that their task is to create two biographical maps—one titled "John Adams: Early Years to the Revolution," the other titled "John Adams: The Post-Revolution Period." Inform students that the maps should be drawn on sheets of butcher paper or posterboard, and each map

should include 10 to 12 significant events or developments in Adams's life. Encourage students to draw inset maps if they find that one or two areas of a map become overcrowded with detail. Remind students that their maps will need certain basic elements, such as a compass rose and a key. Point out that maps will be more informative if they include annotations and captions. Suggest that students start by reviewing the Rubric 20: Map Creation.

5. Conclude by calling on groups to display and discuss their maps. Encourage other students to question group members on why the events and developments shown on their maps should be considered significant.

ASSESSMENT

1. To assess students' biographical maps, use Rubric 20: Map Creation in the *Alternative Assessment Handbook* or in a customizable format on the One-Stop Planner.

2. Additional grades can be based on students' participation in the concluding discussion.

The Expanding Nation

★ ★

BLOCK SCHEDULING LESSON PLANS

THINK ABOUT THEMES

Constitutional Heritage

Agree All branches of government should have an equal balance of power.

Disagree The legislative and executive branches have more responsibilities, and therefore should have more power.

Geography

Agree Settlers will eventually move into new territories and begin exploration.

Disagree A nation should explore new territories in order to establish relations with the people already living there.

Global Relations

Agree The desire for more land will cause neighboring nations to fight.

Disagree Nations along a common border will establish peaceful relations for trade and com-

LESSON 1

(For use with Sections 1 and 2, pp. 334–43)

OBJECTIVES

1. Analyze the views Jefferson expressed about political parties in his first inaugural address.

2. Identify Republican policies Jefferson introduced and the Federalist policies that he accepted.

3. Evaluate the significance of *Marbury* v. *Madison* as an important court case.

4. Describe how and why the Louisiana Purchase took place.

5. Analyze the achievements of the Lewis and Clark expedition, and define the purpose of Pike's expedition.

LET'S GET STARTED!

List the following states on the chalkboard: Arkansas, Colorado, Iowa, Kansas, Louisiana, Minnesota, Missouri, Montana, Nebraska, New Mexico, North Dakota, Oklahoma, South Dakota, Texas, and Wyoming. Ask students what these states have in common. Write students' responses

on the chalkboard and discuss their ideas. Then tell students that all or a part of each of these states was included in the land acquired through the Louisiana Purchase. Tell students that in this lesson they will study the policies of President Thomas Jefferson, most notably the purchase from France of the vast area west of the Mississippi and the exploration of that land.

TEACH OBJECTIVE 1

Level 2: Have a volunteer read aloud the quotation from Thomas Jefferson's first inaugural address on page 335. Discuss with students the message that Jefferson conveyed in his speech. Ask students to write a short paragraph explaining why Jefferson believed his goal as expressed in the address was so important to the United States at that time.

TEACH OBJECTIVE 2

Level 2: Work through the lesson content with students, asking them to list in their notebooks the policies and actions of Jefferson and how Republicans and Federalists responded to these policies and actions. Then organize the class into two groups. Have one group adopt the Republican viewpoint and create a political cartoon that assesses Jefferson's actions as president. Have the other group do the same from the Federalist viewpoint. Ask students to write a paragraph explaining their cartoon and stating their reasons for their viewpoint. **[Cooperative Learning]**

Level 3: Organize the class into two groups to hold a debate. Have one group argue in favor of Jefferson's position about changing government policy to match his ideas and the other side argue in favor of retaining Federalist policies. At the conclusion of the debate, have volunteers summarize the arguments. **[Cooperative Learning]**

TEACH OBJECTIVE 3

Level 1: Instruct students to write a sentence that describes how *Marbury* v. *Madison* and judicial review are linked. **[English Language Learners]**

All Levels: Organize the class into small groups. Ask each group to create "Before and After" images that illustrate the importance of the Supreme Court before it decided the case of *Marbury* v. *Madison,* and its importan from each group to present his or her group's illustrations to the class. **[English Language Learners, Cooperative Learning]**

TEACH OBJECTIVE 4

Level 1: Write the following names on the chalkboard: *Thomas Jefferson, Robert T. Livingston, Charles Talleyrand,* and *Napoléon.* Organize the class into four groups. Assign one historical figure to each group, and ask groups to write a paragraph about their assigned person's major contribution to the Louisiana Purchase. After groups have completed their paragraphs, read them aloud to the class. **[English Language Learners, Cooperative Learning]**

Level 3: Point out to students that the Constitution does not specifically give the federal government the authority to add territory to the United States. Instead, the authority to purchase lands is based on a loose interpretation of the Constitution found in part in interpretations of the elastic clause. Select six students to act as justices on the Supreme Court. (You may wish to remind students that the Supreme Court only had six justices in the early 1800s.) Organize the

other students into two groups. One group will represent the strict constructionist point of view—that the government has no right to purchase new lands. The other group will represent the loose constructionist point of view—that the elastic clause gives the government the right to purchase Louisiana. Have both groups prepare arguments to present to the Supreme Court detailing their positions. Then have the groups present their arguments to the Supreme Court and ask the justices to render a decision. **[Cooperative Learning]**

TEACH OBJECTIVE 5

Level 1: Organize the class in small groups. Give groups a blank map of North America in the early 1800s. On their maps, have groups show the route of Louis and Clark as well as Pike's route. On the backs of the maps, have groups explain why these expeditions were important. **[English Language Learners, Cooperative Learning]**

Level 3: Have students use their textbooks to learn about the lands that the Lewis and Clark expedition explored. Then have them write an article for an abstract that might appear in a scientific or geographical journal. Abstracts might focus on a land formation, a region's climate, or plant and animal life.

REVIEW AND ASSESS

Have students complete the **Sections 1** and **2 Review** questions. Then organize students into groups, and have each group write a short story on one of the following: What might the United States be like if the transfer of power from Adams to Jefferson had not been achieved peacefully? What would the United States be like if it had not acquired the Louisiana Territory? Call on group representatives to read their stories to the class. Then lead a discussion comparing and contrasting the suggestions in the various stories. Finally, have students complete **Daily Quiz 11.1** and **11.2.**

RETEACH

Have students complete **Main Idea Activities for English Language Learners and Special-Needs Students 11.1** and **11.2.** Then have students create a two-column chart on Jefferson's actions as president. Tell students to label the first column *Significant Points of Jefferson's Inaugural Address* and the second column *Actions Taken to Support Jefferson's Plans*. Have students review the lesson to find information to include in the chart. **[English Language Learners]**

EXTEND

Have students use the library to find information about Toussaint-Louverture and the slave revolt he led in Saint Domingue (Haiti). Then ask students write an essay about the revolt's causes, leaders, and results. Encourage volunteers to share their essays with the class. **[Block Scheduling]**

LESSON 2

(For use with Sections 3 and 4, pp. 344–55)

OBJECTIVES

1. Determine why the United States placed an embargo on France and Great Britain.

2. Explain what Tecumseh wanted to accomplish and how successful he was at achieving his goals.

3. Analyze why the United States declared war on Great Britain in 1812.

4. Describe how the war progressed at sea and in the Great Lakes region, and explain how actions taken by American Indians aided the British during the war.

5. Identify the British strategy in the East, and explain how the war ended.

LET'S GET STARTED!

Ask students to identify reasons why nations go to war. Tell students that in this lesson they will learn about three different wars the United States fought in the early years of the nineteenth century—one with the Barbary Pirates, another with American Indians, and the third with Great Britain.

TEACH OBJECTIVE 1

Level 1: Work with the class to create a graphic organizer comparing and contrasting the Embargo Act and the Non-Intercourse Act. After the organizer is filled in, use it to lead a discussion about why the United States passed these laws. **[English Language Learners]**

TEACH OBJECTIVE 2

Level 3: Have students imagine that they are a member of Tecumseh's American Indian confederacy. Tell them that the treaty, signed by General Harrison and some of the Indian leaders, is a sham. Harrison has used every underhanded method available to push you and your people off your land. Other American leaders want you to give up your culture and adapt to the European culture by becoming farmers. You agree with your leader, Tecumseh, that the time has come for the American Indian nations to unite. Tecumseh has sent you as his representative to other Indian groups in an attempt to persuade them to join the confederacy. Have students write a persuasive speech in which they plead with the American Indians to join the confederacy.

Level 2: Have students imagine that they are soldiers in General Harrison's army and that the Battle of Tippecanoe has ended. Have students write a letters to friends in the East explaining how successful Tecumseh and his American Indian confederation have been.

TEACH OBJECTIVE 3

Level 1: Have students review Section 3 to make a list of the events that led to The War of 1812. Write students' answers on the chalkboard. Then lead the class in a discussion of the following question: Did the United States have a legitimate reason for going to war? Why or why not?

TEACH OBJECTIVE 4

Level 2: Give students blank outline maps of North America. Have them create a map depicting significant battles of the war at sea and in the Great Lakes region. Ask students to label each battle, noting the date when each occurred and identifying the victor of each. Also, ask students to add annotations that provide information on interesting events during various battles. Finally, remind students that their maps should include a compass rose, a key, and a title.

Level 3: Ask students to think about the *Chesapeake* incident. Then ask them to create a political cartoon that illustrates how British actions at sea angered Americans.

All Levels: Organize the class into several small groups, and have each group create a series of questions for a quiz game. Assign each group one of the following topics from the textbook: *The War at Sea, American Indians in the War of 1812.* Have students prepare five questions on each assigned topic. Provide students with index cards so that they can write each question on one side of the card with the answer on the other. You may wish to have students assign points for each question—for example, the easiest questions might earn one point and the most difficult five. Then conduct a quiz game using the cards. **[English Language Learners, Cooperative Learning]**

TEACH OBJECTIVE 5

Level 2: Have students create outlines of British strategy in the East and the events leading up to the end of the war. Then have students use this information to write song lyrics for a song about the War of 1812. You may wish to have musically talented students write music to accompany their lyrics.

All Levels: Organize students into small groups, and have each group choose the name of a significant individual involved in the War of 1812 in the East or the end of the war. Give each group several pieces of posterboard and have them create the design for the home page of a Web site about the individual. The main page should contain general biographical information about the individual with links to other pages that contain more specific information. **[English Language Learners, Cooperative Learning]**

REVIEW AND ASSESS

Have students complete the **Sections 3** and **4 Review** questions. Then have them create cause-and-effect flow charts showing the events leading to the War of 1812. The chart should show

how the actions of the British, Native Americans, southerners, and westerners influenced the decision to go to war. Then have students complete **Daily Quiz 11.3** and **11.4.**

RETEACH

Have students complete **Main Idea Activities for English Language Learners and Special-Needs Students 11.3** and **11.4.** Organize the class into groups, and assign each group one of the section's main heads. Have students create a graphic that reflects the content of their assigned subsection. Have groups present their graphics in the order in which the topics appear in the sections. **[English Language Learners]**

EXTEND

Tell students about Dolley Madison's heroic effort to save valuables from the White House in the face of a British attack in August of 1814. Then organize the class into several small groups. Tell each group to conduct research about Dolley Madison's role in the War of 1812. Then have groups use their findings to create a children's book about Dolley Madison. Once the books are created, have groups exchange them and take turns reading the stories. **[Block Scheduling]**

★ ★

TEAM TEACHING STRATEGIES

Journals of the Lewis and Clark Expedition

GOAL

In this activity, students will learn about the Lewis and Clark expedition by writing a journal that might have been kept by Sacagawea, a Shoshone woman who acted as a guide for the expedition.

PLANNING

- **Purpose** This activity may be used in combination with teacher-directed lessons, as an enrichment activity, or as a performance-based assessment of content mastery.

- **Suggested Time** Plan to spend two lesson blocks and one homework assignment on this activity. Provide time for students to read and discuss their journal entries.

- **Teaching Team** At least one social studies teacher and one language arts teacher should take part in teaching this activity.

- **Group Size** This task will work best as an individual assignment. However, students may work in small groups to undertake research.

- **Materials and Resources** Provide students with copies of *Streams to the River, River to the Sea* by Scott O'Dell in addition to copies of Rubric 15: Journals in the *Alternative Assessment Handbook*. Have students use their textbooks to help them find information about Sacagewea and the part she played in the Lewis and Clark expedition.

IMPLEMENTATION

1. Give students an overview of this activity by explaining that they will first read the novel *Streams to the River, River to the Sea* by Scott O'Dell. They will then create a journal that might have been kept by Sacagawea while she acted as a guide for the Lewis and Clark expedition.

2. Lead students in a discussion of the purpose and effect of the Lewis and Clark expedition and Sacagawea's role in making it a success. Then mention that the book that students will read tells the story of Sacagawea's life, putting special emphasis on the part she played in the Lewis and Clark expedition.

3. Next, have students read *Streams to the River, River to the Sea*. As they read, have students consider and note answers to the following questions: How did Sacagawea help the Lewis and Clark expedition? What were her opinions of Lewis, Clark, York, and other members of the expedition? What feelings did she express about the lands the expedition crossed? How did she relate to the American Indian groups with which the expedition came in contact? What were her hopes and fears about the outcome of the Lewis and Clark expedition?

4. When students have completed their reading, tell them that their task is to write a journal of the Lewis and Clark expedition that Sacagawea might have kept. Inform students that journal entries should be based on the notes they made during their reading of *Streams to the River, River to the Sea* and on research they conducted into the Lewis and Clark expedition. Remind students that journal entries should reflect not only what Sacagawea sees but also her feelings and thoughts on events and developments. Suggest that students review Rubric 15: Journals before they begin writing.

5. Call on volunteers to read their journals to the class. Conclude by asking students to discuss how and why a journal written by Sacagawea might differ from one written by Meriwether Lewis or William Clark.

ASSESSMENT

1. To assess students' journal entries, use the Rubric 15: Journals in the *Alternative Assessment Handbook* or in a customizable format on the One-Stop Planner.

2. Additional grades can be based on students' participation in the concluding discussion.

A New National Identity

★ ★

BLOCK SCHEDULING LESSON PLANS

THINK ABOUT THEMES

Global Relations

Agree Nations can resolve land issues through mediation.

Disagree Land is too valuable to surrender without a fight.

Citizenship

Agree In a strong democracy, all people must have the right to vote.

Disagree The military strength of a democracy makes it strong.

Constitutional Heritage

Agree The federal government should not be all-powerful.

Disagree The federal government issues the law of the land, and all states must follow these laws.

LESSON 1

(For use with Sections 1 and 2, pp. 364–73)

OBJECTIVES

1. Examine how the United States settled its land disputes with Great Britain and Spain, analyze President Monroe's reasons for issuing the Monroe Doctrine, and describe its most important points.

2. Discuss the issues that the Missouri Compromise was supposed to address.

3. Analyze how improvements in transportation affected the United States.

4. Explain why the 1824 presidential election was controversial.

LET'S GET STARTED!

Write the word *nationalism* on the chalkboard, and call on volunteers to explain what the term means to them. Ask students to list the reasons why a country's citizens might feel a sense of national pride. Conclude by telling students that in this lesson they will learn how U.S. citizens developed a sense of national pride in the early 1800s.

TEACH OBJECTIVE 1

All Levels: Organize the class into three groups and assign each group one of the following topics: *Rush-Bagot Agreement, Adams-Onís Treaty,* and the *Monroe Doctrine.* Tell students that the U.S. Congress has hired their group to design a billboard that provides information to the American people about its assigned topic. Remind students that their billboards should include visuals and text and should present the information in an eye-catching way. **[English Language Learners, Cooperative Learning]**

Level 3: Ask students to think about the territorial conflicts that took place in the early 1800s between the United States and Great Britain and Spain. Ask students whether they believe these difficulties contributed to the formulation of the Monroe Doctrine. Ask students to write a position paper explaining their views on the subject.

TEACH OBJECTIVE 2

Level 1: Copy the three main conditions of the Missouri Compromise from the text in Section 2 of the chapter. Read through each condition with students, discussing what problems Congress hoped to avoid by passing the Missouri Compromise. **[English Language Learners]**

Level 2: Have students draw political cartoons in support of or in opposition to the Missouri Compromise. Tell students to be sure to include the key points of the Compromise in their cartoons.

TEACH OBJECTIVE 3

Level 1: Point out on a map of the United States Cumberland, Maryland, and Wheeling, West Virginia. Ask students to explain why the federal government decided to build a road between these locations. Then use the map to locate Albany, New York, and Buffalo, New York. Have students explain the benefits that a canal between these cities could bring. Finally, ask students to write a few sentences explaining how improvements in transportation positively affected the United States. **[English Language Learners]**

Level 3: Have students work in groups to build a model of The Cumberland Road or the Erie Canal. Ask volunteers to explain their models to the class. Finally, lead a discussion focusing on how the building of roads and canals improved the nation's infrastructure. **[Cooperative Learning]**

TEACH OBJECTIVE 4

Level 1: Work with students to create a flow-chart showing highlights of the election of 1824. After the flowchart is completed, use it to lead a discussion about how supporters of Andrew Jackson might have felt about President Adams. **[English Language Learners]**

Level 2: Tell students to imagine they are writing an entry for a historical encyclopedia about President Adams's tenure in office. Have students outline the main points of the entry. Outlines should begin with the election of 1824.

REVIEW AND ASSESS

Have students complete the **Sections 1** and **2 Review** questions. Then ask students if they think "The Era of Good Feelings" is an appropriate title for James Monroe's presidency. Suggest that they outline events and developments in Monroe's presidency that support their answers. Finally, have students complete **Daily Quiz 12.1** and **12.2.**

RETEACH

Have students complete **Main Idea Activities for English Language Learners and Special-Needs Students 12.1** and **12.2.** Then tell students that they have been asked by President Monroe to create an outline from the Monroe Doctrine that he can refer to while giving a speech. Have students work individually or in groups to make their outlines. **[English Language Learners]**

EXTEND

Ask students to identify the major development of the Era of Good Feelings they feel will have the greatest impact on life in the United States in 20 years. Direct them to write a paragraph explaining why they think the development they selected will have such significance. **[Block Scheduling]**

LESSON 2

(For use with Sections 3, 4, and 5, pp. 374–88)

OBJECTIVES

1. Examine how Jacksonian Democracy was a sign of change in American politics.

2. Explore how tariff disputes led to the nullification crisis and how President Jackson responded.

3. Describe why President Jackson was against a national bank and how his resistance affected the economy.

4. Explain why the federal and state governments began an American Indian removal policy, examine how American Indians resisted removal and describe how they were affected by removal from their lands.

5. Examine the favorite writers of the early 1800s and what they wrote about, and descibe the focus of the Hudson River School.

LET'S GET STARTED!

Ask students where they believe most American Indians lived prior to 1830, and where they live today. Explain to students that most American

Indians originally lived east of the Mississippi River, but for political and economic reasons, they were forced to move to an area known as Indian Territory, in what is now Oklahoma. Tell students that in this section they will learn about the American Indian removal, as well as Jacksonian Democracy and the new American culture.

TEACH OBJECTIVE 1

Level 2: Write the following statement on the chalkboard: *The Jacksonian era was marked by a growth in democracy.* Then ask students to construct a two-column chart with *Pro* and *Con* as column headings. Direct them to enter in the *Pro* column events and developments that support the statement. Events and developments that challenge the statement should be entered in the *Con* column.
[English Language Learners]

Level 3: Ask students to think about the characteristics of Jacksonian Democracy. Then ask students to write "A Day in the Life of President Andrew Jackson." Students' articles should focus on the political systems he used in running his administration.

TEACH OBJECTIVE 2

Level 1: Write the following names on the chalkboard: *Vice President John C. Calhoun, Senator Daniel Webster, President Andrew Jackson.* Ask students to explain how each of these politicians responded to the nullification crisis.
[English Language Learners]

Level 3: Remind students that Vice President Calhoun supported states' rights. Ask students to take either the point of view of agreeing with Calhoun or opposing him. Then ask students to summarize the tariff disputes as someone holding their opinion might have done at the time.

TEACH OBJECTIVE 3

Level 1: Ask a volunteer to read aloud the quotation from Jackson under the text heading "The Second Bank of the United States" on page 378. Review this quotation with students, making sure that they understand Jackson's vocabulary. Then ask students to paraphrase Jackson's opposition to the bank using their own words.
[English Language Learners]

Level 2: Ask students to create a time line showing the controversy surrounding the Second Bank of the United States. Tell students to include events carried out by supporters of the bank above the time line and to place events carried out by opponents of the bank below the time line.

TEACH OBJECTIVE 4

All Levels: Organize students into four groups and assign each group one of the following topics: *The Indian Removal Act,* Worcester v. Georgia, *The Trail of Tears,* and *The Second Seminole War.* Have each group design and create a mural on their assigned topic. You may wish to have students write a paragraph explaining their mural.
[English Language Learners, Cooperative Learning]

Level 3: Arrange a debate on the following topic: RESOLVED: The United States should have never moved American Indians to reservations. Have students prepare written arguments in support of or in opposition to their assigned viewpoint. Then hold a debate on the topic.
[Cooperative Learning]

TEACH OBJECTIVE 5

Level 1: Have students list the most important characteristics of the Hudson River school. Have students examine a work of Thomas Cole and explain the characteristics they find in it.
[English Language Learners]

Level 2: Have students imagine that they are putting together a museum display on American culture in the early 1800s. Ask them to create the blueprints for this display. Their blueprints should show what/who they will place in their museum and where it will be located. Students should focus on literature and art. You may wish to have students write a paragraph justifying their choices.

REVIEW AND ASSESS

Have students complete the **Section 5 Review** questions. Organize the class into several small groups. Have each group outline the main points in the section. Then have groups exchange their outlines with another group. Have groups fill in supporting information under each section and subsection of the outline. Then have students complete **Daily Quiz 12.3, 12.4,** and **12.5.** **[Cooperative Learning]**

RETEACH

Have students complete **Main Idea Activities for English Language Learners and Special-Needs Students 12.3** and **12.4.** Then have students create a list of events and ideas that reflected the growth of American nationalism. Ask volunteers to read their list to the class. **[English Language Learners]**

EXTEND

Have students choose a work by Washington Irving, James Fenimore Cooper, Catharine Maria Sedgwick, or another American fiction writer of the period. Have them read the selection they chose and then make a gameboard of the story, including the major events and characters. You may wish to tell students that the game will be more interesting if gimmicks such as bonus and bad luck cards are included. **[Block Scheduling]**

A New National Identity

★ ★

TEAM TEACHING STRATEGIES

Poems and Songs of the Erie Canal

GOAL

In this activity, students will learn more about the improvements in transportation made in the 1820s and 1830s by writing songs or poems about the building of the Erie Canal.

PLANNING

- **Purpose** This activity may be used in combination with teacher-directed lessons, as an enrichment activity, or as a performance-based assessment of content mastery.

- **Suggested Time** Plan to spend one lesson block and one homework assignment on this activity. Provide time for students to perform their poems and songs.

- **Teaching Team** At least one social studies teacher and one language arts teacher should take part in teaching this activity.

- **Group Size** This activity works best as an individual assignment. You may choose to assign the activity as an extra credit option for individual students.

- **Materials and Resources** Provide students with copies of the Rubric 26: Poems and Songs in the *Alternative Assessment Handbook* and the novel *We Were There at the Opening of the Erie Canal* by Enid La Monte Meadowcraft. Have students use their textbooks to help them find information about the building of the Erie Canal.

IMPLEMENTATION

1. Give students an overview of the activity by explaining that they will first study the novel *We Were There at the Opening of the Erie Canal* by Enid LaMonte Meadowcraft. They will then write poems or songs that tell about the building of the Erie Canal.

2. Lead students in a discussion about the improvements in transportation made during the 1820s and 1830s, focusing on the construction of the Erie Canal. Then mention that the book that students will read tells of the struggle to complete this artificial water-way connecting Lake Erie to the Hudson River.

3. Next, have students read *We Were There at the Opening of the Erie Canal*. As they read, have them consider and answer the following questions: Who were the workers who built the Erie Canal? What were working conditions like for builders of the Erie Canal? What problems did the workers encounter in building the canal? What are some statistics on the Erie Canal, such as length, width, depth, number of workers involved, and length of time it took to complete? How was the completion of the canal celebrated? What was the impact of the canal on life in Buffalo, New York, and regions to the west? Inform students that if they feel that the novel does not provide sufficient details to answer a particular question, they should use library resources to locate information.

4. When students have completed their reading, ask them to write poems or songs about some aspect of the building of the Erie Canal. Point out that the content of their poems or songs should be based on the notes they took during class discussion and their reading of the novel and on any research they may have undertaken. Suggest that students start by reviewing Rubric 26: Poems and Songs. If students have difficulty getting started, you might play recorded versions of such folk songs as "The Erie Canal" or "John Henry."

5. Conclude by calling on volunteers to sing their songs or recite their poems. Then lead a class discussion about why the completion of great engineering feats is often celebrated through poems and songs.

ASSESSMENT

1. To assess students' poems and songs, use the Rubric 26: Poems and Songs in the *Alternative Assessment Handbook* or in a customizable format on the One-Stop Planner.

2. Additional grades can be based on students' participation in the concluding discussion.

★ ★

BLOCK SCHEDULING LESSON PLANS

THINK ABOUT THEMES

Government

Agree It is the duty of the government to regulate new kinds of technology and transportation.

Disagree Government and business must be kept separate.

Science, Technology & Society

Agree Technology changes the way people work.

Disagree Technology may not affect the work of some people.

Economics

Agree Improvements in transportation strengthen the national economy.

Disagree Developments in transportation might threaten economic stability.

LESSON 1

(For use with Sections 1 and 2, pp. 398–409)

OBJECTIVES

1. Discuss how Samuel Slater contributed to the growth of the textile industry in the Northeast and how Eli Whitney's ideas benefited manufacturing.

2. Describes how events before and during the War of 1812 aided the growth of manufacturing in the United States.

3. Examine how the Rhode Island and Lowell systems differed.

4. List the ways that the introduction of factories influenced the daily life of workers in the northeastern United States.

5. Describe how Sarah G. Bagley and other reformers contributed to the early labor movement.

LET'S GET STARTED!

Call on volunteers to identify appliances and other technological devices that were not available when their grandparents were teenagers. List the responses on the chalkboard. Ask students how their grandparents' lives might have been different if they had had these modern devices. Then ask students to cite advantages and disadvantages of the technological developments they identified and if, overall, life has been made better by such advances. Then tell them that in this lesson they will learn how technological innovations made in the first half of the 1800s changed the nature of work and conditions in factories, on farms, and in cities.

TEACH OBJECTIVE 1

Level 2: Organize the class into pairs, and assign each pair either Samuel Slater or Eli Whitney. Have each pair prepare a question-and-answer interview with its assigned individual. Interviews should focus on their contributions to the development of industry in the United States. Instruct students to base the interviews on material from the section. In each pair, have one partner act as the interviewer and the other as the assigned individual. Call on volunteer pairs to present their interviews to the class. **[Cooperative Learning]**

Level 3: Organize students into two teams. Assign one team to represent Samuel Slater and the other team to represent Eli Whitney. Then challenge teams to debate which man made the greater contribution to the development of American manufacturing and industries. **[Cooperative Learning]**

TEACH OBJECTIVE 2

Level 2: Ask students to create a graphic organizer showing how the War of 1812 contributed to the growth of American manufacturing. Tell students that graphic organizers should include the period directly before and following the war, and should explain the situation that American industries faced during this entire period.

TEACH OBJECTIVE 3

Level 1: Organize students into several groups, and direct each group to create a scrapbook on the Rhode Island and the Lowell systems. Point out that scrapbooks should include pictures, drawings, or sketches of inventions and innovations, factories, factory towns, and prominent individuals. Mention that maps might also be included. Remind students that annotations or captions should accompany illustrations. **[English Language Learners, Cooperative Learning]**

Level 3: Have students use their textbooks to gather information on the Rhode Island and Lowell systems. Then have them create two political cartoons addressing the social and/or economic benefits and drawbacks of each system.

TEACH OBJECTIVE 4

Level 3: Have students imagine that they are employees of the Bureau of Labor and Management and have been asked to do a historical study on the way the Industrial Revolution affected women's work or child labor in factories. Have students use their textbooks to gather information. Then have them present their findings to their supevisor in the form of a memorandum. **[Cooperative Learning]**

TEACH OBJECTIVE 5

All Levels: Have students work in groups to make a flow chart showing the efforts of the early labor movement. Ask groups to present their flow charts to the class. **[English Language Learners, Cooperative Learning]**

Level 3: Have students prepare reports detailing Sarah G. Bagley or another reformer's contribution to the early labor movement.

REVIEW AND ASSESS

Have students complete the **Sections 1** and **2 Review** questions. Then ask students to use the terms listed in the Identify portion of the Section Review to write a half-page report describing the early Industrial Revolution in the United States, using each term at least once. Finally, have students complete **Daily Quiz 13.1** and **13.2.**

RETEACH

Have students complete **Main Idea Activities for English Language Learners and Special-Needs Students 13.1** and **13.2.** Then ask students to write sentences that link the key terms to people, places, and ideas discussed in the lesson, replacing each key term with a blank space. Pair students and have partners exchange their sentences. Then ask students to complete the sentences and return them to their partners for grading. **[English Language Learners, Cooperative Learning]**

EXTEND

Have students design an innovation that streamlines some common classroom task, such as cleaning the chalkboard. Then have students present their designs to the class. Some students may wish to actually build their inventions. **[Block Scheduling]**

LESSON 2

(For use with Sections 3 and 4, pp. 410–19)

OBJECTIVES

1. Describe how the Transportation Revolution changed life in the United States.

2. Discuss the effects of the Supreme Court case *Gibbons* v. *Ogden*.

3. Analyze how the growth of railroads benefited the nation.

4. Describe the ideas Samuel Morse drew upon in order to invent the telegraph.

5. Explain how new developments benefited factory and farm work, and identify the new inventions Cyrus McCormick and Isaac Singer developed.

LET'S GET STARTED!

Ask students to imagine that they have a friend who has moved to another state some 2,000 miles away. Ask them how they might get in touch with their friend to wish him or her happy birthday. Then tell students that they have been invited to their friend's birthday party. Ask them how they might get there. Remind students that today, communication is almost instantaneous and a journey of 2,000 miles can be completed in just a few hours. Then point out that in the early 1800s getting a letter to a friend or visiting a distant town involved a journey that might take weeks, even months. Conclude by telling students that in this lesson they will learn about the revolution in transportation and communication that began to change the way Americans thought about time and travel.

TEACH OBJECTIVE 1

Level 1: On a map of the United States, have students locate and draw the Erie Canal and the Hudson River. Have students create map annotations that explain how canals and steamboats changed life in the United States. **[English Language Learners]**

All Levels: Ask students to list ways that the Transportation Revolution improved life for U.S. citizens. Then organize the class into small groups. Instruct groups to create advertising slogans or jingles that tell how one of these developments will change people's lives. **[English Language Learners]**

TEACH OBJECTIVE 2

Level 1: Discuss with students the significance of the Supreme Court decision in *Gibbons* v. *Ogden*. Then have students create newspaper headlines for a paper that might have reported this decision. **[English Language Learners]**

Level 3: Organize a mock proceeding before the U.S. Supreme Court for the case of *Gibbons* v. *Ogden*. Organize the class into four groups, and assign each group one of the following roles: (a) Gibbons's attorneys (b) Ogden's attorneys, and (c) supreme court justices. Then conduct the proceeding with individuals from the groups playing their respective roles. Encourage members of the Court to ask questions of the attorneys for both sides. At the conclusion of the proceeding, have the judges issue the Court's decision and explain its reasoning. **[Cooperative Learning]**

TEACH OBJECTIVE 3

Level 2: Remind students that Daniel Webster suggested that the railroad towered "above all other inventions of this or the preceding age." Then ask students to evaluate Webster's statement. Have them write a brief paragraph explaining whether or not they agree with Webster.

Level 3: Have students use the textbook to compile data on the growth of railroads between 1830 and 1860. Ask students to look for information such as the total number of miles of track in the United States, train speeds, and the ways that trains were used, in addition to the amount of federal aid provided to assist the growth of railroads. Have students use this data to write an essay analyzing how the growth of railroads benefitted the nation. Have students create charts or graphs depicting the data to include with their essays.

TEACH OBJECTIVE 4

Level 1: Write the following names on the chalkboard: *Alessandro Volta* and *André-Marie Ampère*. Ask students to write a few sentences explaining the relationship between these scientists and Samuel Morse. **[English Language Learners]**

Level 2: Ask students to imagine that they are Samuel Morse. Have them write a letter to Alessandro Volta and André-Marie Ampère thanking these scientists for their contribution to the telegraph.

TEACH OBJECTIVE 5

Level 1: Ask students to think about the new developments and ideas that benefited farm and factory workers, as well as Americans at home. Have students create an illustration showing one of the developments. Ask students to write a caption explaining their illustrations. Encourage volunteers to present their work to the class. **[English Language Learners]**

Level 3: Ask students to imagine that they are critics during the mid-1800s who have been asked to review the new forms of factory and farm technology in the United States. Have students review material from the lesson to evaluate new ideas and developments. Then have students write a review that rates factory and farm technology by using a four-star system. Point out that the review should also include a discussion of each one's advantages and disadvantages.

REVIEW AND ASSESS

Have students complete the **Sections 3** and **4 Review** questions. Then give each student a note card on which is written the name of an invention or technological advance described in this lesson. On the reverse side of the note card, have students describe the purpose of the invention or advance, facts about its creation, details about how it influenced life in the United States, and its advantages over earlier developments. Call on students to read clues on their note cards, and have the rest of the class try to identify the invention or advance. Finally, have students complete **Daily Quiz 13.3** and **13.4.**

RETEACH

Have students complete **Main Idea Activities for English Language Learners and Special-Needs Students 13.3** and **13.4.** Create a chart on the chalkboard with the following column headings: *Invention or Technological Advance, Changes in Lifestyle, Advantages,* and *Disadvantages.* Then ask students to identify the inventions and technological developments discussed in Sections 3 and 4. Enter their responses in the first column of the chart. For each invention, call on volunteers to enter in the appropriate column how it affected life in the United States, its advantages, and its disadvantages. **[English Language Learners]**

EXTEND

Have students use the library to find information about advances in plows and reapers since the mid-1800s. Have students create a series of illustrations depicting how these farm machines have changed over the years. Have students write a brief summary next to each illustration, explaining its improvements over the previous model. **[Block Scheduling]**

★ ★

TEAM TEACHING STRATEGIES

Advice Columns in the 1800s

GOAL

In this activity, students will learn more about working conditions in textile mills by writing advice columns for prospective mill workers.

PLANNING

- **Purpose** This activity may be used in combination with teacher-directed lessons, as an enrichment activity, or as a performance-based assessment of content mastery.

- **Suggested Time** Plan to spend one lesson block and one homework assignment on this activity. Provide time for students to share and discuss their advice columns.

- **Teaching Team** At least one social studies teacher and one language arts teacher should take part in teaching this activity.

- **Group Size** This activity works best as an individual assignment. However, students may work in small groups to undertake research.

- **Materials and Resources** Provide students with copies of *The Lowell Girls*. Have students use their textbooks to help them gather information about working conditions in New England textile mills in the mid-1800s. Also provide students with a copy of Rubric 37: Writing Assignments or Rubric 42: Writing to Inform.

IMPLEMENTATION

1. Give students an overview of the activity by explaining that they will learn more about working conditions in New England textile mills. They will first read an excerpt from the memoirs of Lucy Larcom, who worked in the mills of Lowell, Massachusetts. Then they will write an advice column informing prospective employees about life in the textile mills.

2. Using the text under the headings "Factory Families" and "The Lowell System" as a guide, lead students in a discussion of what life was like for workers in the textile factories of New England. When students discuss the text under "The Lowell System," draw their attention to the information about Lucy Larcom. Inform them that the excerpt they will read is taken from Larcom's memoirs, *A New England Girlhood*.

3. Distribute copies of *The Lowell Girls* to students. Work through the excerpt with them, asking them to consider the following as they read: How did Lucy Larcom view work at the mill at first? What were the regulations that ruled life for workers in the mill? How did mill workers get around some of these regulations? How did workers and mill owners try to make life in the mill more acceptable? Encourage students to take notes as they read.

4. Ask students to imagine that they write the advice column for the *Lowell Offering*. The magazine has received a letter from a girl who is thinking of taking a job at the mill, and she wants to know what life at the mill is really like. Ask students to write a

response to this letter. Point out that their responses should include some basic information like work hours and pay, as well as what they think is good and bad about life at the mill. Suggest that they also include ideas about what the letter writer might do to improve working conditions. Remind students that the content of their columns should be based on the notes they took during class discussion, their reading of the excerpt, and any research they may have undertaken.

5. Conclude by calling on volunteers to read their advice columns to the class. After the readings, lead the class in a discussion of the following: After hearing this advice, would you have wanted to work in a Lowell textile mill of the mid-1800s? Why or why not?

ASSESSMENT

1. To assess students' advice columns, use Rubric 37: Writing Assignments or Rubric 42: Writing to Inform in the *Alternative Assessment Handbook* or in a customizable format on the One-Stop Planner.

2. Additional grades can be based on students' participation in the concluding discussion.

Agricultural Changes in the South

★ ★

BLOCK SCHEDULING LESSON PLANS

THINK ABOUT THEMES

Science, Technology & Society

Agree Many technological advancements are not related to the growth of manufacturing.

Disagree Improvements in technology can be linked to the growth of manufacturing.

Economics

Agree Product specialization can lead to superior quality and knowledge of a product.

Disagree Concentrating on one product limits the ability to adapt to changes in the market.

Culture

Agree Only the predominant group in each region will express its culture.

Disagree Many cultures can exists simultaneously in the same region.

LESSON 1

(For use with Sections 1 and 2, pp. 424–32)

OBJECTIVES

1. Explain what happened to agriculture and slavery in the South immediately after the American Revolution.

2. Analyze the effect of the cotton gin on the South and slavery, and investigate the effects of the cotton boom on the South's economy.

3. Describe how trade and crops other than cotton affected the southern economy.

4. Identify the kinds of factories located in the south.

LET'S GET STARTED!

Present the following scenario to students: On a drive around the city, you see posters and billboards emblazoned with the message *Bob Is King.* You also notice that the majority of the cars on the road have bumper stickers carrying the same message. What do you think the message means? *(Students' responses might be that Bob is a very important person.)* Then inform students that in the mid-1800s many southerners used to say *Cotton Is King.* Tell students that in this lesson they will learn how cotton became "king." They will learn about other crops grown in the South

and how some southerners tried to diversify their economy by building up trade and industry.

TEACH OBJECTIVE 1

Level 1: Tell students that slavery declined in the South immediately after the American Revolution. Write a chart on the chalkboard with the following headings: *Economy* and *Morality*. Tell students to complete the chart with economic and moral reasons that led to the decline of slavery. **[English Language Learners]**

TEACH OBJECTIVE 2

Level 3: Have students imagine that they are northerners traveling in the South in the mid-1800s. Ask them to write journal entries describing cotton's importance to the economy of the South. Tell students they need to address how the cotton gin led to the spread of cotton cultivation across the South and how the growth of the cotton industry affected southern society, particularly the expansion of slavery. Call on volunteers to read their journal entries to the class. Use these readings as the starting point for a discussion on the validity of the statement "Cotton Is King."

Level 1: Work with students to create a cause-and-effect diagram showing how and why the South and sections of the Southwest became more and more dependent on cotton and the slave labor system. Lead the class in a discussion about how this growing dependence on cotton affected the rest of the southern economy. **[English Language Learners]**

TEACH OBJECTIVE 3

Level 2: Have students skim the text for this lesson to identify and note significant information on the economic characteristics of the South other than cotton. Suggest that they focus on the following topics: crops, other than cotton, grown in the South; efforts to encourage trade; and major industries in the South. Then provide students with blank outline maps of the southern United States, and ask them to use the notes they have made to create a map titled *The Economy of the South (1790–1860)*. Point out that the maps need to show where certain crops were grown and the location of major industries. Suggest that the students add annotations to provide further information. For example, one annotation might mention that tobacco was the South's first cash crop. Direct students to write their annotations in boxes that should be attached by leader lines to appropriate points on the map. Remind students that their maps should include a compass rose, a key, and a caption that summarizes the information shown. Reserve about 10–15 minutes for students to display and discuss their maps.

Level 3: Have students use the textbook to find information about the crops produced in the South other than cotton. Have students create a slogan that describes one of these crops importance to the southern economy.

TEACH OBJECTIVE 4

All Levels: Organize students into small groups. Tell each group to imagine that they are an advertising team that has been hired to create a pamphlet for a southern factory. Remind students to include the name of the factory, illustrations, a description of what it produces, its location, and any other relevant information in their pamplets. **[English Language Learners, Cooperative Learning]**

REVIEW AND ASSESS

Have students complete the **Sections 1** and **2 Review** questions. Then organize the class into three groups. Assign each group one of the section's Read to Discover questions. Have each group create a public service announcement that summarizes information about the assigned Read to Discover question. Encourage students to create visual aids to highlight important points. Have each group perform its public service announcement for the rest of the class. Finally, have students complete **Daily Quiz 14.1** and **14.2. [Cooperative Learning]**

RETEACH

Have students complete **Main Idea Activities for English Language Learners and Special-Needs Students 14.1** and **14.2.** Then organize students into small groups. Have each group write a paragraph describing the South's economy. **[English Language Learners, Cooperative Learning]**

EXTEND

Have students use the library to find information about Eli Whitney's cotton gin. Tell them to use their findings to draw an annotated diagram that explains how the cotton gin works. Suggest that students answer the following questions in their annotations: What problem was the cotton gin invented to solve? Who invented it? What year was it invented? What effect did it have on the southern economy and society? Select students to display and discuss their diagrams. **[Block Scheduling]**

LESSON 2

(For use with Sections 3 and 4, pp. 433–43)

OBJECTIVES

1. Describe what life was like for southern planters and owners of small farmers.

2. Analyze what the urban South was like, and examine the challenges free African Americans faced in the South.

3. Explain what work and daily life were like for most slaves, and describe how slaves used family, religion, and other aspects of their culture to help them cope with the slave system.

4. Identify ways that enslaved African Americans challenged the slave system.

LET'S GET STARTED!

Ask students to describe what southern society was like prior to the Civil War. *(Students' responses might be that it had slavery and large plantations.)* Write their responses on the chalkboard. Have students check the accuracy of their descriptions as they work through this lesson.

TEACH OBJECTIVE 1

Level 1: Have students create the cover of a fictional 1850s magazine titled *Southern Society.* Students' magazine covers should in some manner incorporate white planters, farmers, and urban dwellers. **[English Language Learners]**

Level 3: Have students work in small groups to draw maps or blueprints or build models of a typical plantation in the South. Inform students that their maps, blueprints, or models should show the main house, where the planter and his family live; the slaves' quarters; the fields; and any related plantation buildings, such as the overseer's house, the blacksmith's forge, and stables. Call on groups to display and discuss their maps, blueprints, or models. **[Cooperative Learning]**

TEACH OBJECTIVE 2

Level 1: Ask students to recall what economic, legal, and social challenges faced free African Americans in the South. Then organize students into small groups. Have each group select one of these challenges and role-play it for the rest of the class. **[English Language Learners, Cooperative Learning]**

All Levels: Organize students into small groups. Ask each group to create two posters. One poster should illustrate what urban life in the South was like. The second poster should illustrate rural life. Have each group present its poster to the class then lead a discussion on the challenges faced by free African Americans in the South. **[English Language Learners, Cooperative Learning]**

Level 3: Have students think about the lives of free African Americans in the South. Then have them write a poem or song, create a drawing, or

develop a short one-act play describing a typical scenario that might have taken place.

TEACH OBJECTIVE 3

Level 1: Organize students into pairs, and have partners work together to write several sentences that make generalizations about the slave system. Call on pairs to volunteer to share their generalizations with the class. Encourage class members to take notes. Then have pairs use their own sentences and their notes to write a paragraph about society and slavery in the South. **[English Language Learners, Cooperative Learning]**

Level 2: Have students imagine that they have been transported back to southern society in the mid-1800s and now have the opportunity to interview an African slave about his or her life. Ask them to write five questions to ask this person. Then have them write the answers to these questions.

TEACH OBJECTIVE 4

Level 1: Encourage students to look through their textbooks for information about ways that African Americans challenged the slave system. Have students write descriptive words used to describe the treatment of slaves and their attempts to gain freedom. Then have students write several sentences describing slaves' ways of rebelling. Instruct students to use descriptive words from their lists. Encourage volunteers to read their sentences to the class. **[English Language Learners]**

Level 3: Have students imagine that they are newspaper reporters who have been sent to the South to cover Nat Turner's Rebellion. Tell students to begin their articles by discussing ways that enslaved African Americans challenged the slave system. Then have them discuss the rebellion, its outcome, and short- and long-term consequences. You may wish to have students include first-person accounts (either real or fictional) in their articles.

REVIEW AND ASSESS

Have students complete the **Sections 3** and **4 Review** questions. Then rewrite the objectives for this lesson as questions. Organize the class into four groups, and assign each group one of these questions. Have groups create a poem or song that answers their assigned questions. Have a member of each group read or sing the poem or song to the class. Finally, have students complete **Daily Quiz 14.3** and **14.4.** **[English Language Learners, Cooperative Learning]**

RETEACH

Have students complete **Main Idea Activities for English Language Learners and Special-Needs Students 14.3** and **14.4.** Have each student create a list of five questions on lesson content to ask other students. Organize students into pairs and instruct partners to take turns asking each other their questions and correcting one another's answers. Finally, ask students to identify topics from the lesson that they are having difficulty understanding, and lead a discussion on those topics. **[English Language Learners, Cooperative Learning]**

EXTEND

Have each student choose a "plantation novel" to read, such as John Pendleton Kennedy's *Swallow Barn* or Charlotte Howard Gilman's *Recollections of a Southern Matron.* (You may want to provide students with a list of acceptable books to read.) Have students write a book report on the novel. In the report, students should describe how southern society is portrayed in comparison to what students have learned in this section. Ask volunteers to read their reviews to the class and explain their illustrations. **[Block Scheduling]**

Agricultural Changes in the South

★ ★

TEAM TEACHING STRATEGIES

Slave Folktales

GOAL

In this activity, students will learn more about slave culture in the South prior to the Civil War by reading, and then writing, a slave folktale.

PLANNING

- **Purpose** This activity may be used in combination with teacher-directed lessons, as an enrichment activity, or as a performance-based assessment of content mastery.

- **Suggested Time** Plan to spend two lesson blocks and one homework assignment on this activity. Provide time for students to share and discuss their folktales.

- **Teaching Team** At least one social studies teacher and one language arts teacher should take part in teaching this activity.

- **Group Size** This activity works best as an individual assignment. However, students may work in small groups to undertake research. You may wish to assign the activity as an extra-credit option for individual students.

- **Materials and Resources** Have students use their textbooks to help them gather information on slave culture—particularly slave folktales—in the South in the years before the Civil War. Provide students with copies of *The People Could Fly: American Black Folktales* by Virginia Hamilton. You may also wish to provide copies of the Rubric 37: Writing Assignments in the *Alternative Assessment Handbook*.

IMPLEMENTATION

1. Give students an overview of the activity by explaining that they will first read "The People Could Fly" from *The People Could Fly: American Black Folktales* by Virginia Hamilton. Then they will write a similar folktale describing an incident in which the slaves escape or outwit their owners in a way other than flying.

2. Using the text under the heading "Slave Culture" as a guide, lead students in a discussion of African American folktales and their importance to the slaves' way of life. Then inform students that "The People Could Fly" is Virginia Hamilton's retelling of an old slave folktale. Provide students with the following biographical information about Hamilton.

   She was born in Yellow Springs, Ohio, a stop on the Underground Railroad. Her grandfather had settled there after he escaped from slavery in Virginia. Hamilton has written several books for children. One of them, *The House of Dies Drear,* has been dramatized for television. It is a mystery about a boy who moves into a house that once was a station on the Underground Railroad.

3. Have students read "The People Could Fly." As they read, have them consider the following questions: Sarah and the other slaves had long forgotten that they had the power to fly. Why do you think that Sarah and the other slaves remembered about

these powers after so much time? Why do you think the slaveholder denied that the slaves flew away? Why do you think the slaves who were left behind continued to tell the story of Toby and Sarah and the other people who could fly? Identify similar slave folktales that you have read. Encourage students to take notes as they read.

4. Ask students to write a folktale in the style of "The People Could Fly" about slaves escaping to freedom or about slaves outwitting their owners. Remind students that they should draw on the notes they took during class discussion and their reading of the excerpt and on any research they may have undertaken in writing their folktales. Encourage students to illustrate their work with pictures of incidents or characters described in the folktales.

5. Conclude by calling on volunteers to read their folktales to the rest of the class. Then conduct a class discussion on how the telling of folktales might help people cope with living as slaves.

ASSESSMENT

1. To assess students' folktales, use the Rubric 37: Writing Assignments in the *Alternative Assessment Handbook* or in a customizable format on the One-Stop Planner.

2. Additional grades can be based on students' participation in the concluding discussion.

BLOCK SCHEDULING LESSON PLANS

THINK ABOUT THEMES

Citizenship

Agree You should strive to help those who are less fortunate.

Disagree You have no responsibility to help people who are less fortunate.

Economics

Agree Immigration brings people with a desire to succeed, thereby benefiting the economy.

Disagree A strong American economy should help Americans, not people from other countries.

Government

Agree American citizens have the right to work to change laws.

Disagree The laws of the United States were carefully crafted to be fair to everyone.

LESSON 1

(For use with Sections 1 and 2, pp. 452–61)

OBJECTIVES

1. Examine how religion affected Americans during the Second Great Awakening.

2. Describe the transcendentalists' views of American society, and identify some of the ideas of the romantic movement.

3. Explain why so many Irish and German immigrants came to the United States in the 1840s and 1850s, and discuss some Americans' reactions to immigrants.

4. Describe what caused U.S. cities to grow, and analyze the benefits and problems this growth created.

LET'S GET STARTED!

Write the term *Great Awakening* on the chalkboard, and ask a volunteer to explain what it means. *(Students' responses might be that it was a period of religious revival in the mid-1700s.)* Then inform students that they will learn about the Second Great Awakening, new ideas that stirred Americans in the early to mid-1800s, the new waves of immigration, and the growth of cities that took place in the mid-1800s.

TEACH OBJECTIVE 1

All Levels: Ask students to provide a definition for the term *Second Great Awakening*. Tell students that this period of religious revival affected many Americans in many different ways. Then organize students into groups. Have groups chose one effect that the Second Great Awakening had on Americans and create an illustration about it. Remind groups they may choose to focus on one group of Americans, Americans who live in a specific region of the country, or Americans generally. To close, have each group present its illustrations to the class. **[English Language Learners, Cooperative Learning]**

TEACH OBJECTIVE 2

All Levels: Organize students into two groups, and assign each group either transcendentalism or the romantic movement. Have groups create postcards that present important views of members of their assigned movement on their assigned topics. **[English Language Learners, Cooperative Learning]**

TEACH OBJECTIVE 3

All Levels: Organize the class into two groups and tell groups that they have been hired to design a series of posters for museum exhibits commemorating immigration in the United States in the first half of the 1800s. Provide each group with four sheets of butcher paper. Have one group use its butcher paper to create posters for an exhibit titled *Immigration*. Have the other group create posters for an exhibit titled *Reaction to Immigration*. **[English Language Learners, Cooperative Learning]**

Level 2: Have students use the textbook to gather information about immigration to the United States between 1790 and 1860. Have them use their findings to create a series of illustrations showing how and why immigration changed in this period and how some Americans responded. Suggest that they also include maps showing the countries from where the most immigrants came and the areas where the immigrants settled.

TEACH OBJECTIVE 4

Level 1: Organize students into two groups. Ask one group to create a list of the benefits that accompanied the growth of U.S. cities in the mid-1800s. Ask the other group to create a list of the problems that accompanied this growth. Use groups' lists to discuss the changes that took place in cities during this period. To close, ask students to write a brief paragraph explaining whether or not they think the growth of cities was good. **[English Language Learners, Cooperative Learning]**

Level 2: Ask students to imagine that they are visitors from Europe touring the urban centers of the United States in the mid-1800s. Have them prepare a letter to a friend in Europe that describes life in American cities. Have students describe the benefits and problems that urban growth presented.

REVIEW AND ASSESS

Have students complete the **Sections 1** and **2 Review** questions. Then provide each student with several note cards. Instruct students to write 10 questions on the lesson content—one question per card, with the answer on the reverse. Organize the class into pairs and have partners use their questions to quiz each other on lesson content. Finally, have students complete **Daily Quiz 15.1** and **15.2. [Cooperative Learning]**

RETEACH

Have students complete **Main Idea Activities for English Language Learners and Special-Needs students 15.1** and **15.2.** Then organize the class into several small groups, and assign each group one of the subsection headings from Sections 1 and 2. Ask each group to explain their subsection in the form of a comic strip. **[English Language Learners, Cooperative Learning]**

EXTEND

Have each student select an author discussed in this lesson. Have them read a novel, short story, poem, or essay written by their selected author. Have students write a report on the novel, short story, poem, or essay. **[Block Scheduling]**

LESSON 2

(For use with Sections 3, 4, and 5, pp. 462–79)

OBJECTIVES

1. Analyze how reformers improved prisons in the early 1800s, and examine the reasons reformers started the temperance movement.

2. Determine how Americans' educational opportunities changed during the early 1800s.

3. Explore why some Americans became abolitionists, identify ways that abolitionists spread the movement's message, and investigate why some Americans opposed abolition.

4. Explain the effect that the abolition movement had on the women's rights movement.

5. Identify some of the goals of the women's rights movement, and analyze the purpose and significance of the Seneca Falls Convention.

LET'S GET STARTED!

Ask students to identify campaigns to change rules, policies, or laws in which they have been involved or of which they are aware. Then explain to students that in this lesson they will learn about efforts at reform in the 1800s, such as the abolition movement and the womens movement, that resulted in significant changes in American society.

TEACH OBJECTIVE 1

All Levels: Have students prepare posters urging people to attend a meeting to learn about either the prison reform movement or the temperance movement. Invite students to present their posters to the class. **[English Language Learners]**

TEACH OBJECTIVE 2

Level 2: Have students create time lines, covering the years 1780–1890, that include significant events in the history of educational reform in the United States. Tell students that their time lines should include a title and brief annotations explaining the significance of each event on the time line.

All Levels: Organize students into groups, and tell groups to play the role of a magazine design team. The magazine plans to publish a special edition on the educational reform movement, and the students have to design the cover. Suggest that groups brainstorm illustration ideas and then make two or three sketches for cover ideas. Call on volunteers to share their group's work with the class. **[English Language Learners, Cooperative Learning]**

TEACH OBJECTIVE 3

Level 1: Ask students to review their textbooks to find information about the abolition movement. Then organize students into groups and have groups design a series of bumper stickers both supporting and opposing this movement. **[English Language Learners, Cooperative Learning]**

Level 2: Assign each student one of the following individuals: Robert Finley, David Walker, William Lloyd Garrison, Angelina Grimké, Sarah Grimké, Frederick Douglass, Robert Purvis, or Harriet Tubman. Ask students to write a eulogy for their assigned individual that describes his or her contributions to the abolition movement. Remind students that eulogies should explain why this person became an abolitionist.

TEACH OBJECTIVE 4

All Levels: Organize students into small groups. Assign each group either Sarah Grimké or Sojourner Truth. Then have groups write brief biographical sketches in which each woman explains how her involvement in the abolition movement affected her interest and involvement in the women's movement. Ask volunteers to present their sketches to the class. **[English Language Learners, Cooperative Learning]**

TEACH OBJECTIVE 5

Level 1: Organize students into groups. Have groups review Section 5 to identify individuals who made a major contribution to the women's rights movement. Then ask groups to explain each individual's contribution to the movement. Have groups write a brief note to one of these women, describing how his or her contribution has changed American society. **[English Language Learners, Cooperative Learning]**

Level 3: Organize the class into several groups, and tell groups that they are to act as the editorial board of a children's book publisher. Have each group develop a publication plan for an illustrated children's book on the women's rights movement of the mid-1800s. Recommend that groups include the following in their plans: a table of contents, a brief synopsis of each chapter, descriptions of suggested illustrations, and suggestions for entries in a glossary. **[Cooperative Learning]**

REVIEW AND ASSESS

Have students complete the **Section 3, 4,** and **5 Review** questions. Then organize the class into small groups, and assign each group one of the individuals discussed in this lesson. Have groups write three to five questions that they would like to use in an interview of their assigned individual. Have each group ask the class their questions, and call on volunteers to suggest how the interview subjects might have answered. Finally, have students complete **Daily Quiz 15.3**, **15.4,** and **15.5.**

RETEACH

Have students complete **Main Idea Activities for English Language Learners and Special-Needs Students 13.3** and **13.4.** Then have each student create a word puzzle—such as an acrostic puzzle or crossword puzzle—based on significant information from the lesson. Tell them to use key terms, significant events, and important people discussed in Sections 3, 4, and 5 as answers to the clues they write. **[English Language Learners,**

EXTEND

Have students collect old newspapers and magazines. Then ask students to use clippings from newspapers and magazines to create collages titled *Women's Rights—Then and Now.* Inform students that collages should highlight significant advances in women's rights since the movement began. (Students may need to draw some portions of the collages.) **[Block Scheduling]**

New Movements in America

★ ★

TEAM TEACHING STRATEGIES

Underground Railroad Maps

GOAL

In this activity, students will learn about the Underground Railroad by creating a map of the routes that Harriet Tubman followed on her journeys north to freedom.

PLANNING

- **Purpose** This activity may be used in combination with teacher-directed lessons, as an enrichment activity, or as a performance-based assessment of content mastery.

- **Suggested Time** Plan to spend two lesson blocks and one homework assignment on this activity. Provide time for students to display and discuss their maps.

- **Teaching Team** At least one social studies teacher and one language arts teacher should take part in teaching this activity.

- **Group Size** This activity will work best as an individual or small-group assignment. Students may work in small groups to undertake research. However, you may wish to assign this as an extra credit option for individual students.

- **Materials and Resources** Provide students with sheets of butcher paper or poster-board. You might also give students copies of Rubric 20: Map Creation in the *Alternative Assessment Handbook* and copies of *Harriet Tubman: Conductor on the Underground Railroad* by Ann Petry. Have students use their textbooks to help them discover more information about Harriet Tubman and the Underground Railroad.

IMPLEMENTATION

1. Give students an overview of the activity by explaining that they will first study the book *Harriet Tubman: Conductor on the Underground Railroad* by Ann Petry. They will then create a map showing the routes that Harriet Tubman followed on her journeys on the Underground Railroad.

2. Using the text under the heading "The Underground Railroad" as a guide, lead students in a discussion on the Underground Railroad and Tubman's role as a conductor. Then mention that the book that students will read tells of Tubman's own flight to freedom and the many dangerous trips she made back to the South to help other slaves escape. Tell students that the author, Ann Petry, has a very special link to the Underground Railroad—her grandfather fled from a Virginia plantation and took the railroad north to freedom.

3. Next, have students read *Harriet Tubman: Conductor on the Underground Railroad*. As they read, have them consider and note answers to the following: What routes does Tubman follow on her journeys to the North? How large are the parties that Tubman conducts on her journeys on the Underground Railroad? Who runs the stations on the Underground Railroad? How do these people help Tubman and the fugitive slaves? What might happen if they refused to help? How long does an average journey on the Underground Railroad take? What is the final destination for most slaves? Why?

Encourage students to take notes as they read.

4. When students have completed their reading, ask them to draw maps showing some of the routes that Harriet Tubman followed on her trips on the Underground Railroad. Inform students that the maps should be drawn on sheets of butcher paper or poster-board and should include annotations. For example, students might annotate the stops on the Underground Railroad by identifying the people who ran the stops and how these people helped Tubman. Students might also show the approximate distance traveled each day and the approximate distance of the entire route. Remind students that their maps will need certain basic elements, such as a compass rose and a key. Suggest that students start by reviewing Rubric 20: Map Creation.

5. Call on groups to display and discuss their maps. Conclude by conducting a discussion on why people like Tubman and the other Underground Railroad "workers" risked their lives to help others.

ASSESSMENT

1. To assess students' maps, use the Rubric 20: Map Creation in the *Alternative Assessment Handbook* or in a customizable format on the One-Stop Planner.

2. Additional grades can be based on students' participation in the concluding discussion.

THINK ABOUT THEMES

Citizenship

Agree Citizens are free to separate from a government they feel is oppressive.

Disagree Citizens have an obligation to obey the government that they have chosen.

Culture

Agree New foods, languages, traditions, and religions diversify a regional culture.

Disagree Combining cultures threatens a regional identity.

Geography

Agree People seek to settle desirable land.

Disagree Dangerous lands should be left uninhabited.

LESSON 1

(For use with Sections 1, 2, and 3, pp. 488–501)

OBJECTIVES

1. Examine how society was structured in Spanish California, New Mexico, and Texas.

2. Identify the events leading to the establishment of the republic of Mexico, and describe how the Mexican war for independence affected California and Texas.

3. Analyze the reasons why many U.S. settlers in Texas rebelled against the Mexican government.

4. Explain the result of the Texas Revolution.

5. Identify the difficulties American Indians and Tejanos faced in the republic of Texas.

6. Explain what drew new immigrants to Texas.

7. Describe the economic and foreign challenges that faced the Texas government.

LET'S GET STARTED!

Direct students to turn to the map of the Louisiana Purchase on page 340. Have them identify who held much of the lands to the west of the Louisiana Purchase *(Students' answers*

should be Spain). Tell students that in this lesson they will learn about life and rebellion in northern New Spain, the Texas Revolution, and the Republic of Texas.

TEACH OBJECTIVE 1

All Levels: Organize the class into three groups. Assign each group either Spanish California, Spanish New Mexico, or Spanish Texas. Ask groups to create a skit that shows how life was structured in their assigned territory. Have groups present their skits to the class. **[English Language Learners, Cooperative Learning]**

TEACH OBJECTIVE 2

All Levels: On the chalkboard write the first and last entries for a cause-and-effect chart on developments in northern New Spain in the early 1800s—*Father Hidalgo makes the* Grito de Dolores and *Mexico Becomes a Republic.* Ask volunteers to come to the board and add entries to the chart. Then have students write an outline for an article they might write on how developments in northern New Spain in the early 1800s led to independence for Mexico. Inform students that the entries on the cause-and-effect chart could serve as the main headings for their outline. **[English Language Learners]**

TEACH OBJECTIVE 3

Level 2: Organize students into small groups to develop ideas for a pictorial essay on the Spanish West and Southwest. Inform groups that their essays need to cover such topics as the Mexican government's policies toward California and Texas and what changes took place there. **[Cooperative Learning]**

TEACH OBJECTIVE 4

Level 2: Have students develop ideas for designing a quilt titled "Texas Revolution." Inform students that each quilt should be made up of 8 to 10 squares, with each square representing an event, issue, or individual related to its title. Ask students to develop a list of subjects for their squares and ideas for how they might illustrate these subjects.

TEACH OBJECTIVE 5

Level 1: Organize the class into pairs. Have one student in each pair draw a picture illustrating the difficulties that American Indians faced in the Republic of Texas, and the other student draw a picture illustrating the difficulties that Tejanos faced. Have members of each pair exchange their drawings and then create a caption that goes with this illustration. **[English Language Learners, Cooperative Learning]**

Level 3: Ask students to focus on either the problems that American Indians or Tejanos faced in the Republic of Texas. Then have students imagine that they are a member of the group they have selected. Ask students to write an editorial they might write, protesting their treatment under the Republic of Texas government, that might appear in a newspaper of the period.

TEACH OBJECTIVE 6

All Levels: Tell students that narrative poetry—poetry that tells a story—was very popular in the mid-1800s. Organize students into small groups, and have group members work together to write a narrative poem that tells the "story" of why new immigrants came to Texas. **[English Language Learners, Cooperative Learning]**

TEACH OBJECTIVE 7

Level 1: Ask students to think about the problems that the republic of Texas had with its economy and with Mexico. Have students create symbols that stand for these problems. Then ask volunteers present their symbols to the class, and ask the class to guess what these symbols stand for. **[English Language Learners]**

Level 3: Tell students to imagine they are speechwriters for Sam Houston. Ask them to prepare a speech that Houston might have delivered to the citizens of Texas in 1844. Tell students that speeches should focus on the economic and foreign challenges that have faced Texas, and how the Texas government met these challenges.

REVIEW AND ASSESS

Have students complete the **Sections 1** and **2 Review** questions. Then ask students to prepare an annotated time line of events from 1819 through 1836 that led to the independence of Texas. Finally, students complete **Daily Quiz 16.1, 16.2,** and **16.3.**

RETEACH

Have students complete **Main Idea Activities for English Language Learners and Special-Needs Students 16.1, 16.2,** and **16.3.** Then assign students one the key terms in this lesson. Have them write two sentences detailing important information they learned about their assigned key terms. Review each of the terms by calling on volunteers to read their sentences. **[English Language Learners]**

EXTEND

Ask students to read either *Make Way for Sam Houston,* by Jean Fritz, or *I Am Houston,* by Mary D. Wade. Then have them write a biographical sketch of Houston's life from his early years to his involvement in the Texas Revolution. **[Block Scheduling]**

LESSON 2

(For use with Sections 4 and 5, pp. 502–511)

OBJECTIVES

1. Identify the reasons Americans first traveled to the Rocky Mountains and farther west.

2. Explain why Americans settled in Oregon Country, and describe what life was like on the Oregon Trail.

3. Identify the reasons Americans started traveling to California in the early 1800s.

4. Explain why American merchants established a new route to New Mexico.

5. Describe the types of images painted by frontier artists.

LET'S GET STARTED!

Before class, prepare a list of geographic features, trails, and sites of key historical events that will be referred to or discussed in this section. Then point out the location of these places on a large wall map. Finally, tell students that throughout this lesson they will learn how the terms and locations on the list are related to the settlement of the western United States.

TEACH OBJECTIVE 1

Level 1: Write the following headings on the chalkboard: *Mountain Men, Pioneers, Missionaries.* Ask students to explain why each of the these groups traveled west, where they went, and what they did. Write students' responses under the appropriate heading.
[English Language Learners]

Level 2: Organize the class into pairs, and assign each pair one of the following individuals: Manuel Lisan, John Jacob Astor, Jedediah Smith, or Jim Bridger. Have each pair prepare a question-and-answer interview with their assigned individual about why they were interested in the West. In each pair, have one partner act as the interviewer and the other as the assigned individual.
[Cooperative Learning]

TEACH OBJECTIVE 2

Level 2: Tell students that they have been asked to write an entry on Oregon and the Oregon Trail for an encyclopedia of American history. Have students include an appropriate image to accompany their entries.

TEACH OBJECTIVE 3

Level 2: Write the term *Trade* on the chalkboard, and ask students to speculate on the role that trade played in the American expansion into California. Have students support their ideas with information from the lesson.

TEACH OBJECTIVE 4

Level 2: Ask students to imagine they are merchants traveling the trails of the Southwest. Ask students to write several brief journal entries explaining why they are interested in establishing a new route to Mexico.

Level 3: Ask students to imagine that they are investment managers in the mid 1800s attempting to gain support for establishing a route to New Mexico for trade. Have each student prepare a proposal for potential investors in which they explain why such a route would be profitable. Ask volunteers to present their proposals to the class.

TEACH OBJECTIVE 5

All Levels: Organize the class into small groups. Have students imagine that they are putting together an art collection on frontier art. Ask them to create a brochure describing the different paintings that will appear in the collection.
[English Language Learners, Cooperative Learning]

REVIEW AND ASSESS

Have students complete the **Section 5 Review** questions. Then have each student prepare a half-page summary of the lesson, leaving blank spaces for key terms, events, and individuals discussed in the lesson. Then organize students into pairs and have partners exchange their summaries. Students should complete the summaries by filling in the blanks with the correct terms. Finally, have students complete **Daily Quiz 16.4** and **16.5.** **[Cooperative Learning]**

RETEACH

Have students complete **Main Idea Activities for English Language Learners and Special-Needs Students 16.4** and **16.5**. Then have students work independently or in small groups to create a graphic organizer titled "The Former West." Suggest that students focus on four major topics in their organizers—The California Trail, Other Trails to the West, and Artists of the West. **[English Language Learners]**

EXTEND

Have students use the library to find more information on one of the mountain men mentioned in this lesson. Instruct students to use their findings to prepare a brief illustrated report. Encourage students to be creative in the format of their reports. Ask volunteers to share their reports with the rest of the class. **[Block Scheduling]**

TEAM TEACHING STRATEGIES

The Journey West Board Games

GOAL

In this activity, students will learn about traveling on the westward trails by designing an educational board game.

PLANNING

- **Purpose** This activity may be used in combination with teacher-directed lessons, as an enrichment activity, or as a performance-based assessment of content mastery.

- **Suggested Time** Plan to spend six lesson blocks and six homework assignments on this activity.

- **Teaching Team** At least one social studies teacher and one language arts teacher should take part in teaching this activity.

- **Group Size** This activity works best as a small-group project. However, you may wish to assign the activity as an extra credit option for individual students.

- **Materials and Resources** Provide students with copies of *The Pioneers Go West* by George Rippey Stewart and Rubric 14: Group Activity in the *Alternative Assessment Handbook.* Be sure that students have heavy cardboard, scissors, art supplies, and other appropriate materials to create their board games. Have students use their textbooks to help them find information about the trails to the West.

IMPLEMENTATION

1. Give students an overview of the activity by explaining that they will first read the book *The Pioneers Go West* by George Rippey Stewart. They will then create an educational board game based on events discussed in the book that will help other students learn about the trails to the West.

2. Lead students in a discussion of what life was like for pioneers on the journey to the West. Then mention that *The Pioneers Go West* tells the story of an 1844 journey from Council Bluffs, Iowa, along the Oregon Trail to California. Inform students that the book is based on the journal kept by Mose Schallenberger, one of a party of about 50 people who made this trip.

3. Next, have students read *The Pioneers Go West*. As they read, have students consider and write answers to the following questions: (1) What kind of supplies did members of the party take with them? (2) What physical challenges, such as crossing rivers and mountains, did the party confront on its journey west? (3) What other challenges did the party face on the journey? (4) How long did the journey take to complete?

4. When students have completed their reading, organize the class into small groups. Direct the groups to create an educational board game based on the events related in *The Pioneers Go West*. Point out that the object of the game should be to safely bring the party of pioneers from Council Bluffs to California. Encourage groups to create original games, but allow them to base their games, at least in part, on existing board games with which they are familiar. Remind groups that as well as a game board, game cards, and playing pieces, they also will need a title and a set of official rules for their games. Have group members play through their games at least once to check for flaws.

5. Have each group play another group's game. Encourage players to offer constructive criticism of the game to its designers. Conclude by holding a discussion on the value of games as a teaching tool.

ASSESSMENT

1. To assess students' board games, use the Rubric 14: Group Activity in the *Alternative Assessment Handbook* or in a customizable format on the One-Stop Planner.

2. Additional grades can be based on students' participation in the concluding discussion.

★ ★

BLOCK SCHEDULING LESSON PLANS

THINK ABOUT THEMES

Global Relations

Agree Conquering other countries is the best way to gain more land.

Disagree The United States gained Louisiana by purchasing it from France.

Culture

Agree Conflict occurred with American Indians when European settlers first arrived in North America.

Disagree The French and the American Indians encountered each other without conflict.

Geography

Agree Settlers are likely to use resources in the same ways that they did in their old homelands.

Disagree Settlers will adapt to their new environment by using whatever resources are most plentiful.

LESSON 1

(For use with Sections 1 and 2, pp. 516–26)

OBJECTIVES

1. Analyze how Americans' belief in manifest destiny affected western expansion.

2. Explain how the United States acquired Oregon and Texas.

3. Discuss events that led to the Mexican War.

4. Describe Americans' reaction to the declaration of war against Mexico, examine the major battles and events of the war, and explain the terms of the treaty that ended the war.

LET'S GET STARTED!

Have students recall the major topics covered in Chapter 16. *(Students' answers should be U.S. settlement in Texas, the Texas Revolution, and U.S. settlement in the Oregon Country and other areas of the West.)* Then tell students that in this lesson they will learn how the United States acquired large areas of the Southwest and West.

TEACH OBJECTIVE 1

Level 1: Create a two-column chart on the chalkboard with the headings *Supporters* and *Opponents*. Tell students that they will use this chart to list the different groups of people who supported and opposed westward expansion in the 1840s. Then ask students to read the text in Section 1 under the heading "Gone West." When students have finished the reading, ask volunteers to describe groups of people who would belong to each category on the chart. Finally, use the completed chart to lead a discussion of what beliefs Americans' held about manifest destiny and why these beliefs affected western expansion.
[English Language Learners]

Level 3: Have students imagine that they are living in the United States during the 1840s. Have them write a letter to the editor of their local newspaper either supporting or opposing the westward expansion of the United States. Remind students to rely on the idea of manifest destiny to support their answers. Call on volunteers from both sides of the issue to read their letters to the class.

TEACH OBJECTIVE 2

Level 1: Draw a time line on the chalkboard that begins in the 1810s and ends in 1848. Tell students that, as a class, they will use this timeline to fill in events that explain how the United States acquired Oregon. Then call on volunteers to read aloud the first two paragraphs of the text in Section 1 under the heading "Acquiring New Territory." Ask students to volunteer important events in this process, and write these events above the timeline. Then ask students to copy the timeline on a sheet of paper. Have them read the final paragraph silently, and then follow the same process to outline the events that led to the acquisition of Texas. Tell students to write these events below the timeline. **[English Language Learners]**

Level 3: Organize students into small groups, and have groups use their notes to create an outline for a chapter, titled "Westward Expansion," to be included in a U.S. history textbook. Recommend that groups consider the following subjects for inclusion in their chapter outlines: the argument over expansion and its role in the 1844 election; the annexation of Texas and the acquisition of Oregon. Suggest that groups list illustration ideas for the chapter. In addition, have them develop ideas for special features to accompany the chapter, such as "Biography," "Linking Past to Present," "Geography and History," "Global Connections," or "Primary Sources." Have groups share their outlines, illustrations, and special features ideas with the rest of the class. **[Cooperative Learning]**

TEACH OBJECTIVE 3

Level 1: Write the following headings on the chalkboard: *Mexico Responds to the Annexation of Texas, Slidell Goes to Mexico, General Taylor Takes Troops to Mexico, President Polk Speaks to Congress.* Tell students to copy these headings on a piece of paper and to use these headings to help them organize information about the events that led to the Mexican War. Remind students that they should list important events in each category as they read the text in Section 1 under the heading "War Breaks Out." **[English Language Learners]**

Level 3: Organize the class into groups of six. Tell groups that each member should play one of the following roles: President Polk, General

Taylor, Diplomat Slidell, a Mexican official, a Mexican soldier; the sixth student should take on the role of a commentator. Tell students to imagine they are appearing on a news program about the beginning of the Mexican War, and they will share their experiences and thoughts about these events. Encourage participants to respond to each other's ideas. The commentator should direct questions to each of the participants and mediate any disagreements that may arise. **[Cooperative Learning]**

TEACH OBJECTIVE 4

All Levels: Organize the class into several groups, and have each group create a scrapbook on the Mexican War. Remind students that scrapbooks should cover the war's progress and the treaty ending it, as well as Americans' reaction to these events. Tell students that scrapbooks should include maps, sketches of important locations, sketches of battle scenes, pictures of important individuals, and excerpts from newspaper and magazine articles, letters, and speeches. You may also wish to tell students that they may be able to photocopy some of these materials from the textbook, but they will have to construct other materials themselves. Remind students that annotations or captions should accompany scrapbook materials. Encourage groups to display and discuss their scrapbooks. **[English Language Learners, Cooperative Learning]**

Level 3: Give each student an outline map of the United States with state labels. Have them locate and label the territories added to the United States through the Mexican War and the Gadsden Purchase. Direct them to add labels for Spanish place names in these territories. Finally, ask students to give their map a title and write a caption that discusses the extent of Spanish settlement in the present-day United States.

REVIEW AND ASSESS

Have students complete the **Sections 1** and **2 Review** questions. Then draw a chart on the chalkboard with *Territory, When Acquired, How Acquired,* and *Special Points of Interest on Acquisition* as vertical column headings. Have students copy the chart into their notebooks. Then work through the lesson content with students, and have them complete the chart. Finally, have students complete **Daily Quiz 17.1** and **17.2.**

RETEACH

Have students complete **Main Idea Activities for English Language Learners and Special-Needs Students 17.1** and **17.2.** Then write the four lesson objectives in question form on the chalkboard. Organize students into small groups, and have groups write answers to the questions in the form of a song. **[English Language Learners, Cooperative Learning]**

EXTEND

Have students use the library to find information about Saint Patrick's Battalion, a group of Irish American volunteers who fought for Mexico in the Mexican War. Have them present their findings in an oral report that explains why these volunteers chose to fight for Mexico and lists the battles in which Saint Patrick's Battalion was involved. **[Block Scheduling]**

LESSON 2

(For use with Sections 3 and 4, pp. 528–39)

OBJECTIVES

1. Analyze the conflicts caused by new U.S. settlements in the Southwest, and discuss the interaction between various cultures there.

2. Explain why the Mormons moved to the West and what they achieved there.

3. Discuss why many people headed west to California in 1849.

4. Describe what life was like in gold rush mining camps and towns, and analyze how the gold rush changed California.

LET'S GET STARTED!

Ask students to recall why settlers moved west into Texas and the Oregon Country. *(Students' answers should be the opportunity to own land, a chance at a better life, and a desire to spread*

Christianity.) Then inform students that in this lesson they will learn about the Mormons, who traveled west in search of religious freedom, and the forty-niners, who went in search of gold as well as about conflicts caused by this movement West.

TEACH OBJECTIVE 1

Level 3: Have students imagine that they are Californios living in the Mexican Cession in the late 1840s. Have them write a letter to a friend in Mexico describing how their lives have changed since the Mexican War.

All Levels: Organize the class into three groups, and have each group create a series of questions on U.S. settlement in the Southwest for a quiz game. Give students the following guidelines for writing questions: (a) Questions will be organized into the following categories—*Conflicts over Land, Cultural Interactions,* and *Economic Encounters in the Southwest.* (b) Each question will be written on one side of an index card with the answer on the opposite side. Index cards should be sorted according to category. Then conduct the quiz game using the questions developed by the groups. Have two groups compete against each other by answering the third group's questions. Instruct members of the third group to serve as the game's host, scorekeeper, and official panel of judges. Once each competing group has answered several questions, groups will switch roles. The quiz is completed when all three groups have played the role of host. **[English Language Learners, Cooperative Learning]**

TEACH OBJECTIVE 2

All Levels: Organize the class into groups, and tell groups to list 10 items that they might include in a time capsule on the movement westward. Remind students to include items that relate to why the Mormons moved west and what they accomplished there. Ask group representatives to present and explain their time-capsule lists to the rest of the class. **[English Language Learners, Cooperative Learning]**

TEACH OBJECTIVE 3

Level 1: Write the terms *California Gold Rush, forty-niners,* and *prospect* onto the chalkboard. Then ask students to write a sentence that shows how these terms are related. **[English Language Learners]**

Level 2: Ask students to write a biography of a person who might have come to California during the gold rush of 1849. Remind students that biographies should include information about why this person came west, how he or she traveled, and what he or she hoped to find there.

TEACH OBJECTIVE 4

Level 1: Ask volunteers to read aloud the text in Section 4 under the heading "Growth in the West." After each paragraph has been read, ask students to explain the main idea it expressed. After the entire section has been read, ask students to list the most important ways that the gold rush changed California. **[English Language Learners]**

Level 2: Have students write an original song describing life in mining camps and towns in 1849 or 1850. If they want, students might match their lyrics to the tune of a traditional song, or musically inclined students might write a new tune to accompany their song lyrics. Students' songs should include a chorus and at least two verses.

Level 3: Ask students to write a "What If?" story about what California might have been like if the California Gold Rush had not taken place. Tell students to keep in mind the immediate and long-term effects of the gold rush.

REVIEW AND ASSESS

Have students complete the **Sections 3** and **4 Review** questions. Then organize the class into five groups, assigning each group one of the lesson's objectives. Have each group create a drawing or some other form of visual about their objective. Have groups share their work with the rest of the class. Finally, have students complete **Daily Quiz 17.3** and **17.4. [Cooperative Learning]**

RETEACH

Have students complete **Main Idea Activities for English Language Learners and Special-Needs Students 17.3** and **17.4.** Then have students work in small groups to create a study guide for this lesson. Have each group exchange its guide with another group. Group members should then work together to answer the questions included in the study guide. **[English Language Learners, Cooperative Learning]**

EXTEND

Have students use the library to find information on mining techniques or mining camps and towns in the California Gold Rush. Have them use their findings to draw either an annotated diagram of one of the mining techniques or an annotated map of a typical mining camp or town. Encourage students to display their diagrams and maps around the classroom. **[Block Scheduling]**

★ ★

TEAM TEACHING STRATEGIES

Gold-Rush Travel Brochures

GOAL

In this activity, students will learn more about the California gold rush by writing travel brochures for prospective forty-niners.

PLANNING

- **Purpose** This activity may be used in combination with teacher-directed lessons, as an enrichment activity, or as a performance-based assessment of content mastery.

- **Suggested Time** Plan to spend two lesson blocks and one homework assignment on this activity. Provide time for students to present and discuss their travel brochures.

- **Teaching Team** At least one social studies teacher and one language arts teacher should take part in teaching this activity.

- **Group Size** This activity works best as a small-group project. However, you may choose to assign the activity as an extra credit option for individual students.

- **Materials and Resources** Provide students with copies of *West Against the Wind* by Liza Ketchum Morrow and Rubric 29: Presentations in the *Alternative Assessment Handbook.* Have students use their textbooks and the library to help them find information about the California gold rush.

IMPLEMENTATION

1. Give students an overview of the activity by explaining that they will first read the novel *West Against the Wind* by Liza Ketchum Murrow. Tell students that *West Against the Wind* tells the story of Abigail Parker and her journey with her mother and her brother from Missouri to the gold fields of California. Students will then create a travel brochure that offers guidance and advice for other people who are contemplating making the trip to California.

2. Lead students in a discussion about the various routes the forty-niners followed on their journey to California. Have them note the time it took to travel each route and the hardships and dangers each route presented.

3. Next, have students read *West Against the Wind*. As they read, have students note the mode of transportation the Parker family used, the types of supplies they carried with them, the length of time the journey took, the places they stopped along the way, the dangers and hardships they faced, and their arrival in California. Suggest that students use library resources to find more information about the overland and sea routes the forty-niners took to the California gold fields.

4. When students have completed their reading and research, organize the class into groups of four. Tell groups that their task is to create a travel brochure offering guidance and advice for prospective forty-niners. (You might have students study examples of travel brochures before they begin work on this assignment.) Remind groups

that they should include the following in their brochures: maps of the route to California, information on supplies to take and the length of time to allow for the journey, descriptions and pictures of stops on the way and any other places of interest, and information on natural barriers and other hazards and dangers that travelers will face on the journey. Groups also may wish to include brief information about other routes to California. Remind students that their brochures should be based on the notes they made during class discussions and their reading of *West Against the Wind*, and on the research they conducted.

5. Conclude by calling on groups to display and discuss their travel brochures. Encourage students to discuss whether they—like the Parkers—would have been willing to make the journey to the California gold fields.

ASSESSMENT

1. To assess students' travel brochures, use Rubric 29: Presentations in the *Alternative Assessment Handbook* or in a customizable format on the One-Stop Planner.

2. Additional grades can be based on students' participation in the concluding discussion.

THINK ABOUT THEMES

Geography

Agree As a country expands its borders, it causes conflict within that country.

Disagree Peaceful expansion occurs if citizens are reminded of the common good.

Citizenship

Agree The Supreme Court must uphold the Constitution, which guarantees individuals' rights.

Disagree There are some people who are not guaranteed rights under the Constitution.

Constitutional Heritage

Agree Because each state decided to join the Union, any state should be allowed to leave it.

Disagree States should not be able to leave the Union because that would weaken the country.

LESSON 1

(For use with Sections 1 and 2, pp. 552–63)

OBJECTIVES

1. Explain how the outcome of the Mexican War affected the debate over slavery's expansion.

2. Explain the main conditions of the Compromise of 1850 and the views expressed for and against it.

3. Analyze why the Fugitive Slave Act was controversial in the North.

4. Explain how different regions of the country reacted to the Kansas-Nebraska Act, and describe the ways people tried to settle the conflict over slavery in Kansas.

5. Depict the series of violent events that showed the growing division over slavery in the United States.

LET'S GET STARTED!

Write the word *compromise* on the chalkboard, and ask students to recall the role it played in different events in American history. *(Students' answers might be the set of compromises that led to the adoption of the U.S. Constitution and the Missouri Compromise of 1820, which temporarily*

resolved a clash over slavery.) Then inform students that in this lesson they will learn how the government again attempted to resolve the slavery issue through compromise but that growing sectional differences doomed these efforts to failure.

TEACH OBJECTIVE 1

Level 1: On an outline map of the United States, point out the land that made up the Mexican Cession. Ask students why they think that the debate over slavery's expansion heightened after the Mexican War. Then assign each student to represent either a supporter of the Wilmot Proviso or of popular sovereignty. Ask students to create an illustration that shows their group's ideas about the expansion of slavery in the Mexican Cession. **[English Language Learners]**

Level 3: Remind students that according to the Missouri Compromise, slavery was not allowed north of 36°30 latitude but was allowed south of this line. Have students write a persuasive essay about whether or not the Missouri Compromise applies to the Mexican Cession.

TEACH OBJECTIVE 2

Level 1: Organize the class into five groups. Assign each group one of the main conditions of

Henry Clay's plan of the Compromise of 1850. Ask students to write a short, three-paragraph essay. The first paragraph should explain their section of Clay's proposal, the second paragraph should explain any objections to it, and the third paragraph should explain any changes that were made to Clay's proposal in order for the Compromise of 1850 to become law. When groups have completed their essays, ask them to read their work to the class. **[English Language Learners, Cooperative Learning]**

Level 3: Organize students into two debating teams. One team should support the Compromise of 1850 and the other team should oppose it. Then conduct a formal debate. **[Cooperative Learning]**

TEACH OBJECTIVE 3

All Levels: Organize the class into small groups. Ask each group to imagine that they are Northerners opposed to the Fugitive Slave Act who are going to Washington, D.C., to protest against the new law. Have each group create signs and placards that illustrate why the law was controversial in the North. **[English Language Learners, Cooperative Learning]**

Level 2: Have students prepare a book jacket for a novel that might have been written in the 1850s to protest the Fugitive Slave Act. Ask them to include a picture or drawing accompanied by the title on the front cover, a brief summary of the book's contents on the jacket's end flaps, the title, author, and publisher on the spine, and a brief author biography and comments about the book's influence on the back cover.

TEACH OBJECTIVE 4

Level 1: On the chalkboard, construct a two-column chart with the following column-headings: *Supporters of Slavery in Kansas* and *Opponents of Slavery in Kansas*. Review the lesson content from Section 2 with students that covers the Kansas-Nebraska Act and reaction to it. Call on students to suggest events, people, and regions that belonged to each category. Note students' responses in the appropriate column on the chart. **[English Language Learners]**

Level 3: Tell students to imagine they are writing an article for an encyclopedia about the history of

slavery in the United States. Have them write an article about the Kansas-Nebraska Act. Remind students that articles should include events leading up to the act, immediate reaction to the new law, and the responses that people had to it. Encourage students to include appropriate illustrations, maps, or charts with their articles.

TEACH OBJECTIVE 5

Level 3: Point out to students that educated Americans in the mid-1800s often kept journals in which they commented on the affairs of the day. Then direct students to review the text under the heading "Bleeding Kansas." Then have them write brief journal entries on the events they have read about. Remind them that they should write from the viewpoint of someone who wants to see the compromise on slavery continue, someone who supports the abolition of slavery, or someone who supports the expansion of slavery to the new territories.

REVIEW AND ASSESS

Have students complete the **Sections 1** and **2 Review** questions. Then have students create annotated time lines covering the period from the mid-1840s to the mid-1850s that include significant events in the debate over slavery and the admittance of new territories to the Union. Tell students that their time lines should include a title and brief annotations explaining the significance of each event. Finally, have students complete **Daily Quiz 18.1** and **18.2.**

RETEACH

Have students complete **Main Idea Activities for English Language Learners and Special-Needs Students 18.1** and **18.2.** Then organize the class into small groups. Have each group divide the two section materials by subsections among its members. Direct students to write questions about the main ideas presented in their assigned material. Finally, have group members use the questions to quiz one another. **[English Language Learners, Cooperative Learning]**

EXTEND

Have students use the library to find information about the Massachusetts Emigrant Aid Company. Then have them use their findings to create a pamphlet that would encourage northern families to move to Kansas. Pamphlets should include pictures or drawings, brief descriptions of the purpose of migration, and slogans or phrases that capture the goals of the company. Have students share their pamphlets with the class. **[Block Scheduling]**

LESSON 2

(For use with Sections 3 and 4, pp. 564–75)

OBJECTIVES

1. Analyze the effect of the Kansas-Nebraska Act on U.S. political parties.

2. Explain why Dred Scott sued for his freedom and how the U.S. Supreme Court ruled in his case.

3. Examine how Abraham Lincoln and Stephen Douglas differed in their views on slavery.

4. Describe Americans' reactions to John Brown's raid on Harpers Ferry.

5. Analyze the factors that led to Lincoln's victory in the election of 1860 and examine the reasons why some southern states decided to leave the Union.

LET'S GET STARTED!

Ask students to identify events and developments that indicated that slavery was the dominant political issue of the early 1850s. *(Students' responses should be the Compromise of 1850, the Fugitive Slave Act, the publication of* Uncle Tom's Cabin, *the Kansas-Nebraska Act, the events of "Bleeding Kansas," and the beating of Charles Sumner by Preston Brooks.)* Then tell students that in this lesson they will learn that slavery continued to be the central issue in national politics, dividing the nation and ultimately leading to the secession of the southern states.

TEACH OBJECTIVE 1

All Levels: Direct students' attention to the headings in Section 3 entitled "New Divisions" and call on students to identify the significant political events. List their responses on the chalkboard. Then have students use the listed items to create a cause-and-effect chain that ends with Buchanan's election to the presidency. **[English Language Learners]**

TEACH OBJECTIVE 2

Level 2: Have students imagine that they will be interviewing a prominent historian of the Civil War. Have students write five questions that they might ask that historian about the *Dred Scott* case. Then have students exchange their questions, and ask each pair to write the answers to their questions.

TEACH OBJECTIVE 3

All Levels: Have students create a chart that contrasts the views of Abraham Lincoln and Stephen Douglas on slavery. Use completed charts to lead a discussion about these differences and the importance of the Lincoln-Douglas debates. **[English Language Learners]**

TEACH OBJECTIVE 4

Level 1: Read aloud with students the text in Section 4 under the headings "The Raid on Harpers Ferry" and "Judging John Brown." Ask students to note, during the reading, significant events in the raid and the ensuing trial, and create a flow chart of these events on the chalkboard. Use the completed flowchart to lead a discussion about how Americans' reacted to Brown's raid. **[English Language Learners]**

Level 3: Organize the class into small groups. Have groups write a series of newspaper articles about John Brown's raid on Harpers Ferry and American's reactions to it. The first article should focus on the event itself, while successive articles sould describe American's reactions to these events. Encourage students to write an interest-grabbing headline and sketch one or two illustrations to accompany their articles. **[Cooperative Learning]**

TEACH OBJECTIVE 5

Level 1: Write the following names on the chalkboard: *John C. Breckenridge, John Bell, Abraham Lincoln, John C. Crittenden, Jefferson Davis.* Ask students to write a sentence explaining each of these men's role in either the presidential election of 1860 or the secession of the southern states. **[English Language Learners]**

Level 3: Organize students into groups, and tell each group that their task is to create op-ed page headlines for newspapers that might have appeared in the North or the South in 1860. (If students are unclear what an op-ed page is, inform them that it appears *op*posite the *ed*itorial page in a newspaper, and usually consists of articles expressing opinions on important issues.) Mention that the op-ed pages sould focus on the 1860 election and secession. Then have each student select a headline and write the article that accompanies it. **[Cooperative Learning]**

REVIEW AND ASSESS

Have students complete the **Sections 3** and **4 Review** questions. Then have students write a song that summarizes the events leading up to South Carolina's secession from the Union. Finally, have students complete **Daily Quiz 18.3** and **18.4.**

RETEACH

Have students complete **Main Idea Activities for English Language Learners and Special-Needs Students 18.3** and **18.4.** Then organize students into four groups. Give each group a sheet of paper on which one of the following questions is written: Why did Dred Scott sue for his freedom, and how did the U.S. Supreme Court rule on his case? How did Abraham Lincoln's and Stephen Douglas's views on slavery differ? How did Americans react to John Brown's raid? What factors led to Lincoln's victory in the presidential election of 1860, and why did the people of the South decide to leave the Union after the election? Have group members add information on their assigned questions, passing the sheet of paper from one to another in round-robin fashion. When group members feel they have enough information,

have them compose answers to their questions. Call on group representatives to read their answers to the class. **[English Language Learners]**

EXTEND

Have students use the library to find the text of and commentaries on speeches made by Lincoln and Douglas in their debates during the 1858 senatorial election campaign. Ask students to prepare dramatic readings and interpretations of key passages in these speeches. **[Block Scheduling]**

TEAM TEACHING STRATEGIES

Commemorative Stamps for Abraham Lincoln

GOAL

In this activity, students will learn about Abraham Lincoln's life before he became president by creating a series of commemorative stamps.

PLANNING

- **Purpose** This activity may be used in combination with teacher-directed lessons, as an enrichment activity, or as a performance-based assessment of content mastery.

- **Suggested Time** Plan to spend two lesson blocks and one homework assignment on this activity. Provide time for students to display and discuss their stamps.

- **Teaching Team** At least one social studies teacher and one language arts teacher should take part in teaching this activity.

- **Group Size** This activity works best as a group assignment. Groups should number three to five students. However, you may choose to assign the activity as an extra credit option for individual students.

- **Materials and Resources** Have students use their textbooks and any other research materials that will help them learn more about Abraham Lincoln's life before he became president. You might also provide students with copies of the Rubric 3: Artwork in the *Alternative Assessment Handbook* and the play *Abe Lincoln in Illinios* by Robert Sherwood.

IMPLEMENTATION

1. Give students an overview of this activity by explaining that they will first study the play *Abe Lincoln in Illinois* by Robert Sherwood. Students will then create a series of commemorative stamps on Lincoln's life—one stamp for each of the play's 12 scenes.

2. Using students' textbooks as a guide, lead them in a discussion about Abraham Lincoln's early life. Then mention that the play *Abe Lincoln in Illinois* tells Lincoln's story from his early days in Kentucky to the election of 1860.

3. Next, have students read the play. As they read, have students note the major events in Lincoln's life depicted in each of the 12 scenes of the play. Encourage students to use the library to find more information about Lincoln's life. Suggest the following as useful sources: *Lincoln: A Photobiography* by Russell Freedman and *His Name Was Lincoln: A Multimedia Biography* (CD-ROM).

4. When students have completed their reading and research, tell them that their task is to create a series of 12 commemorative stamps celebrating Lincoln's life from his early years to 1860. Suggest that they begin by reviewing the list of events they compiled during their reading of the play. Direct them to select one event from each scene that best sums up Lincoln's life during that period. The stamps should illustrate these

events. Remind students to accompany each stamp with a brief explanation of what it illustrates and why this event is significant.

5. Ask groups to display and discuss their stamps. Conclude by holding a discussion on how Lincoln's life up to 1860 prepared him for the presidency.

ASSESSMENT

1. To assess students' commemorative stamps, use Rubric 3: Artwork in the *Alternative Assessment Handbook* or in a customizable format on the One-Stop Planner.

2. Additional grades can be based on students' participation in the concluding discussion.

BLOCK SCHEDULING LESSON PLANS

THINK ABOUT THEMES

Science, Technology & Society

Agree Technological advances improve one's chances in a war.

Disagree Technology is only one factor in gaining an advantage in war.

Economics

Agree The nation's resources are drained by supporting a war.

Disagree War provides a market for many resources.

Citizenship

Agree Soldiers and civilians have a duty to support their country in war.

Disagree People who disagree with a war's cause should not support it.

LESSON 1

(For use with Sections 1 and 2, pp. 580–89)

OBJECTIVES

1. Describe what led to the bombardment of Fort Sumter, and explain why this event was important.

2. Identify which side of the conflict Arkansas and the Upper South joined and why, as well as why both the North and the South wanted to claim the border states.

3. Analyze the strategies each side followed at the beginning of the war.

4. Analyze why the battles the Confederates won in Virginia were important and explain what stopped their northward advance.

5. Examine the significance of the *Monitor* and the *Virginia*.

LET'S GET STARTED!

Have students imagine that they are President Abraham Lincoln in 1861. Ask them how they would handle the challenge of bringing the Confederate states back into the Union without going to war. Then tell students that in this lesson they will learn that Lincoln's efforts to maintain the Union and prevent the outbreak of war failed. Also, they will learn about each side's early strategies and early battles of the war.

TEACH OBJECTIVE 1

All Levels: Discuss with the students the significance of the bombardment of Fort Sumter. Ask students to draw on this discussion and design posters encouraging volunteers to join the Union or Confederate armies. Call on volunteers to present and explain their posters to the class. **[English Language Learners]**

TEACH OBJECTIVE 2

Level 1: Have students work in small groups to create a bulletin-board display of a map of the United States in 1861. On the map they should show the states that remained loyal to the Union and the states that joined the Confederacy. Have students also identify the border states and the Upper South. **[English Language Learners, Cooperative Learning]**

TEACH OBJECTIVE 3

All Levels: Ask students to explain the strategies that the North and the South followed at the beginning of the war. Students may create compare and contrast charts, make drawings, or write an essay that describes these different strategies. **[English Language Learners]**

Level 3: Organize the class into two groups. Tell the members of one group that they are advisers to President Lincoln and members of the other group that they are advisers to President Davis. Have each student write a memo to his or her respective president advising the president on military strategy. Remind students to include speculation regarding the response that the proposed strategy might have on the other side in the conflict. Ask volunteers to share their strategies with the class.

TEACH OBJECTIVE 4

Level 2: Bring copies of *Calliope, Cobblestone, Scholastic Update,* and other similar young people's magazines to class. Organize students into small groups, and encourage groups to use these periodicals to develop ideas for a young people's magazine of their own. The magazine would cover the early battles in Virginia and Maryland. Recommend that groups analyze the two battles at Bull Run, the Seven Days Battles, and the Battle of Antietam. **[Cooperative Learning]**

TEACH OBJECTIVE 5

Level 2: Ask students to write a brief assessment of the war at sea. Tell students that in making their assessments they should focus on the battle between the *Monitor* and the *Virginia.*

REVIEW AND ASSESS

Have students complete the **Sections 1** and **2 Review** questions. Then have them write a two-paragraph summary of the lesson content, one paragraph for Section 1 and one paragraph for Section 2. Have students complete Daily Quiz **19.1** and **19.2.**

RETEACH

Have students complete **Main Idea Activities for English Language Learners and Special-Needs Students 19.1** and **19.2.** Then draw a chart on the chalkboard with the following

vertical column-headings: *North* and *South.* Use the following as horizontal column-headings: *States, Resources, War Strategies,* and *Battle Victories Through 1862.* Ask students to copy and complete the chart. **[English Language Learners]**

EXTEND

Have students use the library to find information about one of the battles discussed in this lesson. Have them present their findings in visual form, using diagrams, charts, graphs, or sketches. **[Block Scheduling]**

LESSON 2

(For use with Sections 3 and 4, pp. 590–99)

OBJECTIVES

1. Examine General Ulysses S. Grant's strategy for the Union army in the West, and explain why the fall of Vicksburg, Mississippi was important.

2. Describe the fighting that took place in the Far West.

3. Determine how different groups in the North reacted to Abraham Lincoln's Emancipation Proclamation.

4. Identify the ways that African Americans and women contributed to the war effort.

5. Explain how northerners and southerners responded to the new draft laws.

LET'S GET STARTED!

Ask volunteers to identify Civil War battles with which they are familiar with from books, movies, or television programs. As students identify battles, point out the location of each battle on a large map of the United States. Tell students that in this lesson they will learn that several major battles and some important developments took place in the West. They also will learn about the contributions of African Americans and women to the war effort and the opposition to the war in both the North and the South.

TEACH OBJECTIVE 1

Level 2: Have students imagine that they are a Confederate soldier. Have them write a first letter to their family about the battles and strategy to gain control of the Mississippi River. Then have them write another letter telling them about the fall of Vicksburg.

TEACH OBJECTIVE 2

Level 1: Organize students into small groups, and tell each group that they are working on a project to create a Web site on the Civil War. Give groups several sheets of butcher paper, and tell them that their task is to create Web pages titled "War in the West." Point out that each home page should contain general information on the topic with links to other pages where more specific information might be found. Have groups design, illustrate, and write information for both pages. In addition, ask groups to create samples for some of the linked pages. **[English Language Learners, Cooperative Learning]**

TEACH OBJECTIVE 3

Level 2: Remind students that northerners viewed the Emancipation Proclamation in different ways. Ask students to write a newspaper article focusing on their different reactions to the Proclamation. Encourage students to include quotes in their articles.

TEACH OBJECTIVE 4

All Levels: Organize the class into small groups. Have students create a medal honoring either the contributions of African Americans or women to the war effort. Ask groups to write a brief message they would give the recipient along with the medal. **[English Language Learners, Cooperative Learning]**

Level 3: Remind students that Abraham Lincoln issued the Emancipation Proclamation under his authority as president in time of war. Ask students to write an essay in which they identify how different groups in the North responded to the Emancipation Proclamation and examine the reasons these groups responded in the ways they did.

TEACH OBJECTIVE 5

Level 2: Organize the class into an equal number of groups. Assign half the groups the topic "Northerners and the Draft," and the rest of the groups the topic "Southerners and the Draft." Have groups imagine that they are living at the time of the Civil War and plan to organize a protest to these new draft laws. **[Cooperative Learning]**

REVIEW AND ASSESS

Have students complete the **Sections 3** and **4 Review** questions. Then organize students into small groups. Have groups review the material in **Sections 3** and **4.** Then for each major heading in the two sections have groups write a sentence that states the main idea of the paragraphs under that heading. Have students complete **Daily Quiz 19.3** and **19.4. [Cooperative Learning]**

RETEACH

Have students complete **Main Idea Activities for English Language Learners and Special-Needs Students 19.3** and **19.4.** Create an outline for lesson content that has several blank spaces where names or concepts should be located. Make copies of the outline and distribute them to students. Have students complete the outlines by filling in the blanks. **[English Language Learners]**

EXTEND

Have students use the library to find information about Civil War battles in which African Americans played a major role. Have them use their findings to write a short story from the viewpoint of an African American soldier involved in the battle. **[Block Scheduling]**

LESSON 3

(For use with Section 5, pp. 600–605)

OBJECTIVES

1. Examine why the Battle of Gettysburg was important.

2. Identify the campaigns that were launched in Virginia and the Lower South.

3. Explain how and when the war finally ended.

LET'S GET STARTED!

Write the term *turning point* on the chalkboard, and ask students to explain its meaning. *(Students' responses might be it is a point at which a major change takes place.)* Then tell students that in this lesson, they will learn about the Battle of Gettysburg, a major turning point in the war. They also will learn about the Union's drive to victory and the Confederate surrender in 1865.

TEACH OBJECTIVE 1

All Levels: Organize the class into three groups. Ask each group to create an annotated map that illustrates one day in the Battle of Gettysburg. Remind students that their maps should include a compass rose, legend, and annotations that describe the events that took place on each day of the battle. Have volunteers from each group present the maps to the class and use them to lead a class discussion on why the Battle of Gettysburg was important. **[English Language Learners, Cooperative Learning]**

Level 3: Have students create a dialogue that might have taken place between General George Pickett and General Robert E. Lee after the Battle of Gettysburg was over. Each speaker should explain why his side's victory or loss is significant and predict how this battle will affect the outcome of the war.

TEACH OBJECTIVE 2

Level 1: Give students a blank outline map of the United States, and have them create a map titled "The Civil War (1864)." Tell students that they need to locate the campaigns launched in Virginia and the Lower South. Have them add brief annotations to provide additional information. **[English Language Learners]**

Level 3: Organize the class into several groups, and provide each group with 5 sheets of butcher paper. Have groups use the sheets of butcher paper to create 5 frames for a filmstrip titled "the North's Drive Toward Victory (1864)." Make sure that groups understand their filmstrips should focus on campaigns in Virginia and the Lower South. Inform students that the frames might be maps, pictures, graphs, charts, diagrams, cartoons, or written materials. **[Cooperative Learning]**

TEACH OBJECTIVE 3

Level 2: Have students write a brief epitaph for the Confederacy. The epitaph should explain its path to defeat in 1865.

REVIEW AND ASSESS

Have students complete the **Section 5 Review** questions. Then have students create a graphic organizer titled "The End of the War, 1863–1865." Suggest that they divide their organizers into three sections—*Events, People Involved,* and *Consequences.* Have students display and explain their completed graphic organizers. Finally, have students complete **Daily Quiz 19.5.**

RETEACH

Have students complete **Main Idea Activities for English Language Learners and Special-Needs Students 19.5.** Ask students to work in small groups to create a study guide, including questions, for this lesson. Have each group exchange its guide with another group. Group members should then work together to answer the questions included in the study guide they received. **[English Language Learners, Cooperative Learning]**

EXTEND

Have students use the library to find statistics on the costs of the Civil War—for example, the dollar amount the North and the South spent on fighting the war, casualties for each side (including a breakdown of battle deaths and deaths from disease), and the destruction in the North and South (buildings destroyed, miles of railroad track ripped up, and so on). Have students present their findings in a chart. **[Block Scheduling]**

★ ★

TEAM TEACHING STRATEGIES

Civil War Museum Exhibits

GOAL

In this activity, students will learn about the Civil War by creating museum exhibits on events and developments that took place from 1860 to 1865.

PLANNING

- **Purpose** This activity may be used in combination with teacher-directed lessons, as an enrichment activity, or as a performance-based assessment of content mastery.

- **Suggested Time** Plan to spend two lesson blocks and two homework assignments on this activity. Provide time for students to present and discuss their museum exhibits.

- **Teaching Team** At least one social studies teacher and one language arts teacher should take part in teaching this activity.

- **Group Size** This activity works best as a small-group project. However, you may choose to assign this activity as an extra credit option for individual students.

- **Materials and Resources** Have students use their textbooks and any other research materials to help them find information about the Civil War. You may wish to provide students with copies of *Across Five Aprils* by Irene Hunt, as well as copies of Rubric 22: Multimedia Presentations in the *Alternative Assessment Handbook*.

IMPLEMENTATION

1. Give students an overview of the activity by explaining that they will first read the book *Across Five Aprils* by Irene Hunt. They will then design museum exhibits titled "One Family's War."

2. Lead students in a discussion about the major events and developments of the Civil War including the seesawing military fortunes of the North and the South. Also, have students discuss what life was like for people on the home front as well as for those on the battlefront. Then mention that *Across Five Aprils* tells the story of the Creightons and how they are affected by the Civil War.

3. Next, have students read *Across Five Aprils*. As they read, have students consider and note how each of the family members is affected by the Civil War. Specifically, have them record the battles and other events in which various family members are involved. You might suggest the following books as appropriate sources of information: *The Civil War Source Book* by Philip Katcher and *War, Terrible War* by Joy Hakim.

4. When students have completed their reading and research, organize them into small groups. Direct groups to design a museum exhibit titled "One Family's War." Point out that the exhibit should be housed in a room about the size of the classroom and should tell the story of the Creighton family across the five Aprils of the Civil War. Tell groups that their exhibit designs should include a floor plan of the exhibit room, noting where various items will be displayed, and a detailed list of items to be displayed, which might include excerpts from letters; photographs; pictures; sketches; maps, newspaper and periodical clippings; contemporary and modern books on the Civil War; uniforms, weapons, and other equipment used by the armies; and stills from movies and documentaries about the Civil War. Remind students that the museum exhibit materials should be based on the notes they made during class discussions, their reading of *Across Five Aprils,* and the research they conducted.

5. Have groups display and discuss their exhibit materials. Ask presenters to explain why groups selected certain events to illustrate and why they chose particular items as illustrations of these events. Conclude by asking students to discuss if—and how—the experience of the Creightons during the Civil War was typical of American families.

ASSESSMENT

1. To assess students' museum exhibit designs, use Rubric 22: Multimedia Presentations in the *Alternative Assessment Handbook* or in a customizable format on the One-Stop Planner.

2. Additional grades can be based on students' participation in the concluding discussion.

★ ★

BLOCK SCHEDULING LESSON PLANS

THINK ABOUT THEMES

Constitutional Heritage

Agree As our society changes, so should our Constitution.

Disagree The Constitution is thorough and should remain intact forever.

Government

Agree A civil war would not have occurred if the previous government had been a strong one.

Disagree A civil war does not indicate a poor existing government.

Culture

Agree Cultural expression, such as art and literature, often reflects changing political ideas.

Disagree Political changes do not effect the culture or the expression of culture in a society.

LESSON 1

(For use with Sections 1 and 2, pp. 620–32)

OBJECTIVES

1. Analyze the effect that the end of the Civil War had on African Americans in the South.

2. Contrast the views of Abraham Lincoln, Congress, and Andrew Johnson on Reconstruction.

3. Explain how Black Codes restricted African Americans' freedom.

4. Analyze the reasons that Radical Republicans tried to impeach President Johnson.

5. Describe the Republicans' efforts to protect the civil rights of African Americans.

LET'S GET STARTED!

Ask the class to imagine a house that has been knocked down by a powerful storm. Have students explain whether they would use similar materials to rebuild the house so that it would look exactly like the original, or whether they would revise the design in various ways. Discuss the advantages of each approach with the class. Explain to students that after the Civil War, the United States had to decide how to

rebuild and that various groups differed on how to reconstruct the nation. Conclude by telling students that these differences led to conflicts between the president and Congress.

TEACH OBJECTIVE 1

Level 1: Have students use their textbooks to gather information about life for African Americans in the South immediately following the Civil War. Tell students to use this information to create a banner titled "Changes in the South." On their banners, students should explain what life in the South was like for African Amercans right after the war. **[English Language Learners]**

Level 3: Have students think about what the lives of African Americans in the South were like before the Civil War and what their lives were like immediately after it ended. Ask students to write a compare and contrast essay focusing on how southern African Americans' lives changed from one period to the next.

TEACH OBJECTIVE 2

Level 1: Write these headings on the chalkboard: *President Abraham Lincoln, Congress,* and *President Andrew Johnson.* Read aloud with students the text from Section 1 that focuses on the

Reconstruction plans presented by each of these people or groups. Invite students to suggest details about these plans throughout the reading, and write students' suggestions on the chalkboard under the appropriate heading. Use the completed chart to lead a discussion comparing and contrasting these views. **[English Language Learners]**

Level 3: Assign students to represent one of the following people: Lincoln, Johnson, or a member of Congress. Then have each student write a diary entry from his or her person's point of view that describes their view about Reconstruction and explains what is wrong with opposing ideas.

TEACH OBJECTIVE 3

Level 2: Have students imagine that they are reporters for a northern magazine who have been sent to the South. Tell students to write a half-page article that describes the implementation of the Black Codes and how they restricted the freedoms of African Americans.

TEACH OBJECTIVE 4

Level 1: Ask students to volunteer reasons why the Radical Republicans wanted to impeach President Johnson. List students' correct responses on the chalkboard. After all the reasons have been given, divide the class into five groups and assign each group one of the reasons. Have groups write a speech they might have presented to Congress—focusing only on their assigned reason—to convince members to impeach Johnson. **[English Language Learners, Cooperative Learning]**

Level 3: Tell students to imagine they are a member of Congress voting on whether or not to impeach Johnson. Ask students to write a short paper explaining how they voted and why.

TEACH OBJECTIVE 5

All Levels: Organize students into small groups. Have each group imagine that they are Republican members of a congressional commission developing a plan to protect the civil rights of African Americans. Tell students to draw up a list of suggestions of how this goal could be

accomplished and implemented. **[English Language Learners, Cooperative Learning]**

Level 3: Review with students the efforts taken by Republicans to protect the civil rights of African Americans. Then have students write a paragraph predicting the outcome of civil rights in the south based on this progress.

REVIEW AND ASSESS

Have students complete the **Sections 1** and **2 Review** questions. Then ask students to think of five questions about the lesson and write each question on a note card. Divide the class into two teams. Have students play a few innings of Review Baseball. Have each team establish a "batting" order. Ask the first student a question. If he or she answers the question correctly, it counts as a hit and the student advances to first base. Have students that reach a base move to the next base each time a teammate correctly answers a question. A run is scored when a person crosses home plate. An incorrect answer counts as an out. Once a team has three outs, the other team takes a turn answering questions. Repeat this process as many times as you wish but allow teams an equal number of turns. Finally, have students complete **Daily Quiz 20.1** and **20.2. [Cooperative Learning]**

RETEACH

Have students complete **Main Idea Activities for English Language Learners and Special-Needs Students 20.1** and **20.2.** Then organize the class so that every student has a partner. Have one student in the pair state everything he or she knows about one of the following topics: African Americans in the South after the war; the Reconstruction plans of Lincoln, Johnson, and Congress; the Black Codes; the Radical Republicans; and the impeachment of President Johnson. The second student should take notes on what the other student says. When finished, the person taking notes should add any information that may have been overlooked by his or her partner. Students should take turns repeating this until each topic has been covered. **[English Language Learners, Cooperative Learning]**

EXTEND

Remind students that many women's rights activists were disappointed that the Fifteenth Amendment did not grant women the right to vote. Have students use the library to gather information about how some women's rights activists (e.g., Elizabeth Cady Stanton, Carrie Chapman Catt, Susan B. Anthony, Sarah and Angelina Grimké, and Sojourner Truth) responded to the amendment's failure to grant women the right to vote. Then have students use this information to write a one-page report showing women's reactions to this subject. **[Block Scheduling]**

LESSON 2

(For use with Sections 3 and 4, pp. 633–43)

OBJECTIVES

1. Describe the reforms Reconstruction governments carried out.

2. Analyze the factors that led to the end of Reconstruction and examine how southern laws and goverments changed after Reconstruction ended.

3. Describe how southern agriculture changed after the Civil War.

4. Analyze why some business leaders hoped to create a "New South."

5. Discuss some popular forms of southern culture during and after Reconstruction.

LET'S GET STARTED!

Ask students to discuss the definition of the term *revolution.* Explain to them that many people viewed Reconstruction as an attempt to achieve an economic, political, and social revolution in the South. Encourage students to consider whether they agree or disagree with this view as they work through the following lesson.

TEACH OBJECTIVE 1

All Levels: As a class, have students create a list of reforms Reconstruction governments carried out. Then divide the class into small groups and assign one reform to each group. Have groups write an encyclopedia article explaining how their assigned reform benefitted the South. **[English Language Learners, Cooperative Learning]**

TEACH OBJECTIVE 2

Level 1: Work with the class to create a time line, beginning in 1872 and ending in 1877, that shows the events that led to the end of Reconstruction. After the time line is completed, have students copy it on a sheet of paper. Tell students to write a one-sentence annotation explaining the significance of each entry on the time line. **[English Language Learners]**

Level 3: Tell students to imagine they are African Americans living in the South in the post-Reconstruction years. Have students write a letter to the president protesting the way African Americans are now being treated in the South as a result of new laws and new local governments.

TEACH OBJECTIVE 3

Level 2: Organize the class into pairs. Have students take on the role of a southerner who was a sharecropper in the late 1800s and is being interviewed by an historian. Have one student tell his or her history while the other writes down the story. Then have them switch roles. Have students use this information to write a short monologue about the life of a sharecropper in the late 1800s. **[Cooperative Learning]**

TEACH OBJECTIVE 4

All Levels: Organize the class into small groups. Tell group members to imagine that they are respected community members in the South during Reconstruction. Have groups create a chart that shows the advantages of industry over agricultural work. After groups have completed their charts, have them write a paragraph explaining why they recommend the creation of a "New South." **[English Language Learners, Cooperative Learning]**

TEACH OBJECTIVE 5

Level 1: Tell students to imagine they are a historian working on a book about life in the South after the Civil War. Have students write an introduction for a chapter about popular forms of southern culture. Remind students to be sure to mention the important topics and themes raised in southern literature and music. **[English Language Learners, Cooperative Learning]**

Level 1: Assign students the name of one of the following writers: Charles W. Chesnutt, Anna Julia Cooper, George Cable, Joel Chandler Harris, Mary Noailles Merfree, or Mark Twain. Have students create a stamp that illustrates the work for which their writer is best known. **[English Language Learners]**

REVIEW AND ASSESS

Have students complete the **Sections 3** and **4 Review** questions for these sections. Then draw their attention to the words and terms in the Define and Identify sections. Ask them to create a list of definitions by using a brief phrase to describe each word or term. Then have students scramble the list to create an activity involving matching the words or terms in each list to the definitions. Have each student exchange his or her activity with a classmate. Each student should then complete the activity and give it back to the student who wrote it for grading. Finally, have students complete **Daily Quiz 20.3** and **20.4. [Cooperative Learning]**

RETEACH

Have students complete **Main Idea Activities for English Language Learners and Special-Needs Students 20.3** and **20.4.** Organize the class into groups. Explain to students that the government wants them to evaluate the success or failure of Reconstruction. Have the groups review material from this section and from class notes to determine their opinion on the subject. Each group should write a summary of its findings that explains the reasoning behind its opinion. **[English Language Learners, Cooperative Learning]**

EXTEND

Ask students to locate a short story by an author discussed in this section or lyrics from an African American spiritual. Tell students to imagine they are entertainment critics assigned to write a review of the chosen work. Reviews should explain how accurately the story or spiritual reflects the lives and values of southerners during this period, as well as the changes in society that occurred after the Civil War. Have students use a four-star rating system with one star representing a poor review and four stars representing an excellent review. **[Block Scheduling]**

★ ★

TEAM TEACHING STRATEGIES

The Effects of Jim Crow Laws

GOAL

In this activity, students will learn about life for African Americans in the South after Reconstruction by writing a poem that describes the effect of Jim Crow laws.

PLANNING

- **Purpose**   This activity may be used in combination with teacher-directed lessons, as an enrichment activity, or as a performance-based assessment of content mastery.

- **Suggested Time**   Plan to spend two lesson blocks and one homework assignment on this activity. Provide time for students to offer each other feedback on their finished poems.

- **Teaching Team**   At least one social studies teacher and one language arts teacher should take part in teaching this activity.

- **Group Size**   Because of the personal nature of poetry, this activity will work best as an individual assignment. However, students may work in small groups to undertake research.

- **Materials and Resources**   Provide individual students with copies of the poem "Jim Crow Cars" by Lizelia Augusta Jenkins Moorer. You might also provide students with copies of Rubric 26: Poems and Songs in the *Alternative Assessment Handbook*. Have students use their textbooks, the library, and any other research materials that will help them find information about segregation in the South after Reconstruction.

IMPLEMENTATION

1. Give students an overview of the activity by explaining that they will write a poem about segregation in the South after Reconstruction.

2. Using the information under the heading "The Era of Jim Crow" as a guide, lead students in a discussion about the elimination of Reconstruction reforms and the introduction of segregation and Jim Crow laws. Then distribute copies of the poem and the rubric to students.

3. Point out that Lizelia Augusta Jenkins Moorer lived and worked as a teacher in South Carolina in the late 1800s and early 1900s. Mention that this poem is taken from her book *Prejudice Unveiled and Other Poems*, which was published in 1907. Then work through the poem with students, asking them to consider the following questions as they read: What do you think Moorer meant by "legalized humiliation"? What are some examples of the humiliation suffered by African Americans on trains in the South? What happened if African Americans complained about this treatment? What is the mood of the poem? Why do you think Moorer chose to write in this way? As students discuss these points, encourage them to take notes.

4. Next, review the rubric with students, pointing out that it lists the basic requirements for writing a good poem or song. Then ask students to begin work on their poems.

Suggest that they start by undertaking research on segregation and Jim Crow in the South in the late 1800s and early 1900s. Also, encourage them to locate and study other poems by African Americans on this subject. When they have completed their research, ask students to write their poems. Remind them to follow this writing procedure: plan before writing; write a first draft; review and revise the first draft; edit and proofread the work; write a final neat copy.

5. Conduct a concluding discussion on Jim Crow laws by calling on volunteers to read their poems to the rest of the class. Encourage students to critique poems as they are presented.

ASSESSMENT

1. To assess students' poems, use Rubric 26: Poems and Songs in the *Alternative Assessment Handbook* or in a customizable format on the One-Stop Planner.

2. Additional grades can be based on students' participation in the concluding discussion.

★ ★

BLOCK SCHEDULING LESSON PLANS

THINK ABOUT THEMES

Economics

Agree The government must fund business development so people in underdeveloped regions can prosper.

Disagree Businesses and people in underdeveloped areas are responsible for creating their own prosperity.

Culture

Agree One group always imposes its cultural beliefs and customs upon another.

Disagree Different groups live peacefully by sharing resources and learning about each others' cultural beliefs and customs.

Geography

Agree People form communities to survive and prosper within difficult environmental conditions.

Disagree The difficulty of facing harsh environmental conditions is not worth the possibility of failure.

LESSON 1

(For use with Sections 1 and 2, pp. 648–54)

OBJECTIVES

1. Identify the animals the Plains Indians used and explain why they were important.

2. Explain the causes and results of conflicts between American Indians and American settlers in the West, and describe how the reservation system and the Dawes Act affected the American Indians.

3. Describe some of the the challenges of mining in the West.

4. Examine the obstacles the builders of the transcontinental railroad faced, and evaluate how it affected the settlement and development of the West.

LET'S GET STARTED!

Ask if anyone in the class has ever had to move to another city or state because of a parent's

job. Encourage students who have moved to discuss how they felt about moving and to identify how their lives have changed as a result of the move. Explain to students that in this section they will learn how the U.S. government forced the Plains Indians to leave their lands and how their lives changed as a result.

TEACH OBJECTIVE 1

Level 1: Ask students to name the two animals on which the Plains Indians depended for survival. Then ask students to draw a series of pictures showing how the Plains Indians made use of the horse and the buffalo. **[English Language Learners]**

Level 2: Tell students that Plains Indian culture was damaged greatly by the disappearance of the buffalo. Have students write an obituary about the death of the buffalo and the effect this has had on Plains Indians.

TEACH OBJECTIVE 2

Level 1: Organize the class into small groups and give each group an outline map of the United States. Have students highlight the American West. Ask them to locate and identify places where conflicts took place between American Indians and American settlers. Finally have students write map annotations explaining the causes and results of these conflicts. **[English Language Learners, Cooperative Learning]**

Level 2: Have students draw a two-column chart on a piece of paper. On the lefthand side of the start, students should list what supporters of the Dawes Act hoped the new reservation system would accomplish. On the righthand side of the chart, students should list how the reservation system actually affected American Indians.

Level 3: Organize the class into small groups and assign each group one of the Plains Indians groups discussed in these sections. Then tell students that they are to take part in a meeting of all the Plains Indian groups to decide how they will respond to the continued encroachment of white settlers on their lands. Have students write a treaty that their group might have given to the U.S. government. In their treaty, students should explain their Plains Indian group's current situation, the course of action they plan to take, why they think this is the best plan, and what they want the U.S. government to do. **[English Language Learners]**

TEACH OBJECTIVE 3

Level 2: Tell students to imagine they are miners in the West. Have them write a letter to friends or family back east, describing their lives in the mining towns and the challenges their job poses.

Level 3: Organize the class into small groups. Have groups use their textbooks to find information on the difficulties associated with mining in the West. Then have groups use the information they find to prepare a short television news documentary on their topic. Each group should create and use appropriate visuals in their documentaries. Have groups tape or perform their news documentaries for the class. **[Cooperative Learning]**

TEACH OBJECTIVE 4

All Levels: Organize the class into small groups. Assign half the groups the role of railroad workers and the other groups the role of railroad company owners. Then have each group write a short narrative describing the problems they faced in completing the transcontinental railroads. Encourage each group to use details from the textbook in their stories. **[English Language Learners, Cooperative Learning]**

Level 2: Write the following term on the chalkboard: *railroads*. Then have students draw cause-and-effect graphic organizers explaining how this term is related to the settlement and development of the West.

REVIEW AND ASSESS

Have students complete the **Sections 1** and **2 Review** questions. Then have students work in pairs to create annotated time lines about the wars between the Plains Indians and the Amercian settlers in the West, the growth of mining and mining towns, and the building of the transcontinental railroad. Finally, have students complete **Daily Quiz 21.1** and **21.2.**

RETEACH

Have students complete **Main Idea Activities for English Language Learners and Special-Needs Students 21.1** and **21.2.** Then turn the objectives for this lesson into questions and write them on the chalkboard. Have students use their textbooks to write an answer to each question. **[English Language Learners]**

EXTEND

Organize students into small groups. Have each group design an advertisement that might have appeared in an eastern newspaper calling for Pony Express riders. Advertisements should include a job description and necessary skills. Have students decorate their advertisements with a map and appropriate illustrations. Have each group present its ads to the class. **[Cooperative Learning, Block Scheduling]**

LESSON 2

(For use with Sections 3 and 4, pp. 656–67)

OBJECTIVES

1. Identify the factors that led to the the cattle boom, and describe what life was like for cowboys.

2. Analyze the causes of the Cattle Kingdom's decline.

3. Identify the groups that settled the Great Plains and examine their reasons for moving there.

4. Discuss how the environment of the Great Plains affected settlers' farming methods.

5. Describe what life was like on the Great Plains for settlers and how they adapted to the conditions.

LET'S GET STARTED!

Ask students to describe what they think the life of a cowboy or a farming family on the Great Plains was like, based on their impressions from watching television and movies. Explain to students that while some of what they see in the media about cowboys and farm life on the Great Plains is accurate, much of it is misleading or exaggerated. In this lesson, they will learn about life on the Great Plains.

TEACH OBJECTIVE 1

Level 2: Have students create a comic strip that explores the rise of the cattle boom. Ask volunteers to present their comic strips to the class. Then lead a discussion about the factors that led to the cattle boom.

Level 3: Have students write descriptions for the job of a cowboy that might have appeared in a newspaper at that time. Tell students that their job descriptions should include an overall description of the job's responsibilities as well as descriptions of a cowboy's duties.

TEACH OBJECTIVE 2

Level 1: Ask students to brainstorm a list of the factors that might cause a cattle ranch to fail.

Write their answers on the chalkboard. Then ask students to look through their textbook to find the reasons the Cattle Kingdom ended. **[English Language Learners]**

Level 3: Have students write a brief biographical sketch of a fictional cattle ranch owner whose ranch fails. Ask volunteers to present their biography to the class.

TEACH OBJECTIVE 3

Level 1: Assign each student one of the following groups of people: farmers from the East or Midwest; single women; African American Exodusters; or European immigrants. Tell students to imagine they are a member of that group who has recently settled on the Great Plains. Have students write a few sentences explaining where they came from and why they relocated. **[English Language Learners]**

Level 2: Have students create an illustrated poster advertising land for sale on the Great Plains. Tell students to remember the reasons people migrated to the Great Plains and to address one or more of these reasons in their advertisement. In addition, advertisements should include information about land values and opportunities.

TEACH OBJECTIVE 4

Level 2: Review the Define terms from Sections with students. Then organize the class into small groups and have each group write a short story or fable in which they use each of the Define terms explaining how the environment of the Great Plains affected settlers' farming methods. **[English Language Learners, Cooperative Learning]**

All Levels: Organize the class into small groups. Ask each group to imagine that they work for the Department of Agriculture and that it is their job to create an illustrated pamphlet that describes the environment of the Great Plains and steps that farmer's can take to adapt their farming methods to that environment. **[English Language Learners, Cooperative Learning]**

TEACH OBJECTIVE 5

Level 2: Have students use their textbook to find information about a farming town in the Great Plains in the late 1800s. Then have students use this information to write a short paper describing life in these towns and how settlers adapted.

REVIEW AND ASSESS

Have students complete the **Sections 3** and **4 Review** questions. Then have students create a crossword puzzle using the Define terms from these two sections. Students should exchange their puzzle with another student in the class. After students complete the other's puzzle, have them check each other's work. Finally, have students complete **Daily Quiz 21.3** and **21.4.**

RETEACH

Have students complete **Main Idea Activities for English Language Learners and Special-Needs Students 21.3** and **21.4.** Then ask students to think about the daily challenges that ranchers, cowboys, and farmers in the West faced. Students should adopt the role of one of these people and write a letter to a friend detailing the challenges they face and how they cope with them. Ask volunteers to present their letters to the class. **[English Language Learners]**

EXTEND

Organize the class into small groups and have each group research education on the Great Plains during the mid- to late 1800s. Have students find out what schools were like and what topics students studied. Suggest that students use the library and first-hand accounts of life in the 1800s in their research. Have groups present their findings to the class in an oral presentation. Encourage students to create visual aids to accompany their presentations. **[Cooperative Learning, Block Scheduling]**

★ ★

TEAM TEACHING STRATEGIES

Cowboy Tall Tales

GOAL

In this activity, students will learn about life in the Cattle Kingdom by investigating and writing reports about tall tales about cowboys.

PLANNING

- **Purpose**   This activity may be used in combination with teacher-directed lessons, as an enrichment activity, or as a performance-based assessment of content mastery.

- **Suggested Time**   Plan to spend two lesson blocks and one homework assignment on this activity. Provide time for students to offer each other feedback on their finished reports.

- **Teaching Team**   At least one social studies teacher and one language arts teacher should take part in teaching this activity.

- **Group Size**   This activity works best as a small-group project. However, you may choose to assign the activity as an extra credit option for individual students.

- **Materials and Resources**   Provide students with copies of the poem "They Have Yarns" by Carl Sandburg. Have students use their textbooks and other research materials to help them find information about legends and tall tales about cowboy life as well as its reality. You may wish to provide students with copies of Rubric 37: Writing Assignments in the *Alternative Assessment Handbook*.

IMPLEMENTATION

1. Give students an overview of the activity by explaining that they will first study a poem about American tall tales and then write a report that compares tall tales and legends about cowboys with the reality of life on the cattle ranges and cattle trails.

2. Lead students in a discussion about the rise and fall of the Cattle Kingdom and the lifestyle of cowboys.

3. Distribute copies of the poem and inform students that Carl Sandburg was not only a poet but also a folksinger. In searching for songs to perform, he discovered a wealth of information about American folktales and legends. Before students read the poem, point out that a tall tale, or yarn, is an exaggerated story that is usually not believable. As they read the poem, ask students to note any tall tales they recognize or any that remind them of others that they know. Continue by asking students to identify any tall tales or yarns that they know about cowboys or life on the cattle range. Write their responses on the chalkboard.

4. Organize students into several groups and ask group members to select two or three items from the list on the chalkboard. Have some group members conduct research on these and other yarns. Have the rest of the group research what life was really like for cowboys working on the cattle range and on the cattle trails. Have group members

combine their research to write a one-page report titled "Cowboy Life: Myth and Reality." Encourage groups to illustrate their reports with appropriate visual materials.

5. Conclude the discussion on cowboy life by asking groups to present their reports to the rest of the class.

ASSESSMENT

1. To assess students' reports, use Rubric 37: Writing Assignments in the *Alternative Assessment Handbook* or in a customizable format on the One-Stop Planner.

2. Additional grades can be based on students' participation in the concluding discussion.

Modern America

★ ★

BLOCK SCHEDULING LESSON PLANS

THINK ABOUT THEMES

Global Relations

Agree Nations in conflict resolve issues through warfare.

Disagree Compromises and treaties have resolved many issues between nations in conflict.

Citizenship

Agree A government should allow citizens to disagree with it.

Disagree Citizens should support their government.

Economics

Agree Global economic development is a responsibility of all nations.

Disagree A nation should focus on promoting its own economic development without relying on other countries.

LESSON 1

(For use with Sections 1 and 2, pp. 682–687)

OBJECTIVES

1. Describe the changes in industry and business that took place in the late 1800s and explain the effects of industrialization on factory workers and farmers.

2. Analyze how progressives addressed the nation's social and political problems.

3. Examine how U.S. foreign policy changed in the late 1800s and early 1900s.

4. Describe the technological and cultural changes that shaped life in the United States after World War I.

5. Analyze how President Franklin D. Roosevelt tried to solve the economic problems brought on by the Great Depression.

LET'S GET STARTED!

Ask students to volunteer words, terms, people, or events that they think best describes the United States from the late 1800s through the 1940s. Remind students to think about daily life, economic changes, and foreign affairs. List students' replies on the chalkboard. Allow students time to study all the suggestions. Then ask them to use these suggestions, as well as their own ideas, to write a brief description of the United States from the late 1800s through the 1940s. Tell students that in this lesson they will learn about changes in industry and business, reform efforts, World War I and post-war society, and the Great Depression.

TEACH OBJECTIVE 1

Level 2: Write the terms free *enterprise* and *Sherman Antitrust Act* on the chalkboard. Ask students to define these terms. Then ask them to explain how these terms illustrate changes in industry and business that took place in the late 1800s.

Level 3: Pair students. Assign each pair either the role of factory workers or farmers. Have students create a dialogue between the pair, focusing on the changes people in their profession have experienced in the late 1800s because of industrialization. Invite pairs to present their dialogues to the class. **[Cooperative Learning]**

TEACH OBJECTIVE 2

All Levels: Create a four-column chart on the chalkboard with these headings: *Political*

Reforms, Social and Labor Reforms, Racial Reforms, Economic Reforms. Ask students to fill in the chart with as much information as they can about these progressive reform movements. Remind students to include key organizations, people, laws, and reform activities. **[English Language Learners]**

TEACH OBJECTIVE 3

Level 2: Tell students to imagine they are a presidential advisor. Ask students to write a memo to the president outlining the changes that took place in U.S. foreign policy in the late 1800s and early 1900s and analyzing the results of this change in policy. Encourage students to include suggestions for future foreign policy.

TEACH OBJECTIVE 4

All Levels: Organize the class into small groups. Provide each group with five sheets of butcher paper and have groups use the sheets of butcher paper to create five frames for a filmstrip on the technological and cultural changes that shaped the United States after World War I. **[English Language Learners, Cooperative Learning]**

TEACH OBJECTIVE 5

Level 3: Have students write a newspaper article analyzing President Hoover's and President Roosevelt's efforts to bring an end to the Great Depression. Remind students that newspaper articles should include facts, statistics, and quotes.

REVIEW AND ASSESS

Have students complete the **Sections 1** and **2 Review** questions. Then have students write 10 questions about Sections 1 and 2 on individual note cards with the answers on the reverse side. Divide students into groups and have them use their note cards to question the other members of the group. Have students complete **Daily Quiz 22.1** and **22.2. [Cooperative Learning]**

RETEACH

Have students complete **Main Idea Activities for English Language Learners and Special-**

Needs Students 22.1 and **22.2.** Have students take out the description they wrote during the Let's Get Started! activity and revise them. **[English Language Learners]**

EXTEND

Have students work in groups of four to research various elements of the free silver issue in the late 1800s. Groups should concentrate on topics such as (1) the monetary history of the country since the 1830s, including legislation that affected federal purchase of gold and silver; (2) the economic problems faced by farmers at the end of the 1800s; (3) farm cooperatives and the subtreasury plan; and (4) the concept of free and unlimited coinage of silver and why farmers expected it to solve their economic problems. Have each member of each group use the library and other resources to find information on one of the topics and decide how best to present the information to the class. After students have created their portions of the group's presentation, have each group present its material to the class. **[Block Scheduling]**

LESSON 2

(For use with Sections 3 and 4, pp. 695–706)

OBJECTIVES

1. Explain how the United States contributed to an Allied victory in World War II.

2. Identify how the Cold War influenced U.S. foreign policy.

3. Analyze what American society was like in the 1950s.

4. Describe the foreign policy issues faced by Presidents Kennedy and Johnson while they were in office.

5. Define the achievements of the 1960s civil rights movement and identify the domestic challenges the United States faced in the early 1970s.

LET'S GET STARTED!

Ask a volunteer to read Winston Churchill's "iron curtain" statement. Then tell students that in this lesson they will learn that the struggle described by Churchill between the two competing ideologies dominated U.S. foreign policy for more than 40 years after World War II. Add that they will also learn about the major social developments and challenges in the United States in the 1960s and 1970s.

TEACH OBJECTIVE 1

Level 1: Write the following headings onto the chalkboard: *Advantages, Disadvantages.* Ask students to volunteer, using one or two words only, what advantages and disadvantages the United States had when it entered World War II. Write students' responses in the appropriate columns. Organize students into pairs, and ask each pair to create an illustration that demonstrates how the United States was able to overcome its disadvantages and contribute to an Allied victory in World War II.

TEACH OBJECTIVE 2

All Levels: Ask student what word or terms they think best defines the Cold War. Write students' suggestions on the chalkboard. Then ask them what words or terms they think best defines U.S. foreign policy in the 1940s and 1950s. Write students' suggestions on the chalkboard. Finally, direct students to this lesson's second Read to Discover question. Ask students to use the appropriate words and terms listed on the chalkboard to answer this question. **[English Language Learners]**

TEACH OBJECTIVE 3

Level 2: Organize the class into small groups. Tell students that they are television executives working on the development of a documentary about American society in the 1950s. Have each group develop an outline for their programs, including a title, a brief overview of the content, individuals and events they would like to focus on, visual ideas, and people they would like to interview. **[Cooperative Learning]**

TEACH OBJECTIVE 4

Level 3: Organize the class into groups of five to six. Have each group create a multimedia presentation about the foreign policy issues faced by Kennedy and Johnson. **[Cooperative Learning]**

TEACH OBJECTIVE 5

All Levels: Organize students into groups of three to five. Tell groups that they have been hired to design a mural titled *A Time of Change: American Society in the 1960s and 1970s.* Tell students to focus on the civil right movement and other social challenges. Have groups decide what developments, events, people, and places they intend to include in the mural. Next, have groups make a rough sketch of the whole mural. They should then break the mural down into several sections and make more detailed sketches of those sections. **[English Language Learners, Cooperative learning]**

REVIEW AND ASSESS

Have students complete the **Sections 3** and **4 Review** questions. Then prepare 20 to 25 review cards on the content of this lesson. Organize the class into three or four teams to play a quiz game. Ask the teams questions in turn until all the question cards have been used. Award one point for a correct answer. Finally, have students complete **Daily Quiz 22.3** and **22.4**. **[Cooperative Learning]**

RETEACH

Have students complete **Main Idea Activities for English Language Learners and Special-Needs Students 22.3** and **22.4**. Rewrite the objectives for this lesson as questions. Have students write answers to these questions using the terms and individuals listed in the Identify segment of the Section 3 and Section 4 Reviews. **[English Language Learners]**

EXTEND

Have students use the library to find information on U.S. involvement in the Korean and Vietnam wars. Then have students use their findings to write a report that compares U.S. involvement in these two conflicts. **[Block Scheduling]**

LESSON 3

(For use with Section 5, pp. 707–711)

OBJECTIVES

1. Explain how the Cold War progressed in the 1980s.

2. Examine the legislative successes and failures of the Clinton administration.

3. Analyze how the United States took part in world affairs in the 1990s.

LET'S GET STARTED!

Write the words *Democrat* and *Republican* on the chalkboard. Ask students to list words that describe each term; write their responses under the appropriate heading on the chalkboard. Explain to students that in this lesson they will learn about the successes and failures of the Reagan, Bush, and Clinton administrations and how their policies affected U.S. citizens.

TEACH OBJECTIVE 1

Level 1: Work with students to create a time line on the chalkboard titled The Cold War, 1980s. Then ask students to select one of these events and write a brief explanation of its significance. Ask volunteers to add their explanations to the time line. **[English Language Learners]**

TEACH OBJECTIVE 2

Level 2: Have students issue report cards on the Reagan, Bush, and Clinton administrations. Students should first decide what foreign and domestic policies and issues they are going to evaluate and then give that issue or policy a grade. Then have each student write a paragraph evaluating the overall success or failure of each president's administration. Call on volunteers to present their paragraphs to the class.

All Levels: Organize students into small groups. Tell each group to imagine that it is a production company for a motion picture studio that is considering making a movie about the Clinton years. Ask each group to create a storyboard that illustrates the legislative successes and failures of the Clinton administration. Ask volunteers to present their storyboards to the class. **[English Language Learners, Cooperative Learning]**

TEACH OBJECTIVE 3

Level 1: Organize the class into small groups. Have groups create wall maps of the world that show conflicts in which the United States was involved in the 1980s and 1990s. **[English Language Learners, Cooperative Learning]**

Level 3: Have students write an opinion piece analyzing the U.S. role in world affairs in the 1990s. Remind students that an opinion piece draws on facts but expresses the writer's personal response to these facts, as well as the author's thoughts and ideas.

REVIEW AND ASSESS

Have students complete the **Section 5 Review** questions. Then draw a chart on the chalkboard with *Reagan, Bush, Clinton, and Bush* as vertical column headings and *Domestic Policy Actions* and *Foreign Policy Actions* as horizontal column headings. Have students copy and complete the chart. Finally, have students complete **Daily Quiz 22.5.**

RETEACH

Have students complete **Main Idea Activities for English Language Learners and Special-Needs Students 22.5.** Then have students work in pairs to create a crossword puzzle using key terms, significant events, and important individuals discussed in the lesson. Have pairs exchange puzzles, and direct partners to work together to complete the puzzle they have received. **[English Language Learners, Cooperative Learning]**

EXTEND

Have students use the library to find information about the fall of the Berlin Wall. Then have students imagine that they are witnessing this event and have them write an eyewitness account. Call on volunteers to present their accounts to the class. **[Block Scheduling]**

Modern America

★ ★

TEAM TEACHING STRATEGIES

Internment Camp Memorials

GOAL

In this activity, students will learn more about Japanese American internment during World War II by designing memorials for those who were sent to the detention camps.

PLANNING

- **Purpose** This activity may be used in combination with teacher-directed lessons, as an enrichment activity, or as a performance-based assessment of content mastery.

- **Suggested Time** Plan to spend two lesson blocks and one homework assignment on this activity. Provide time for students to present and discuss their memorial designs.

- **Teaching Team** At least one social studies teacher and one art teacher should take part in teaching this activity.

- **Group Size** This activity works best as a small-group project. However, you may choose to assign the activity as an extra credit option for individual students.

- **Materials and Resources** Provide students with copies of *Journey to Topaz* by Yoshiko Uchida. Have students use their textbooks, the library, and other research materials to help them find information about Japanese American internment during World War II and on various memorials, such as the Lincoln Memorial and the Vietnam Veterans Memorial. You may wish to provide student with Rubric 3: Artwork in the *Alternative Assessment Handbook*.

IMPLEMENTATION

1. Give students an overview of the activity by explaining that they will first read the book *Journey to Topaz* by Yoshiko Uchida. They will then design memorials for those Japanese Americans who were held in detention camps.

2. Lead students in a discussion of Japanese American internment during World War II. Then tell students that *Journey to Topaz* is the story of Yuki Sakane and her family, who are removed from their home in California and sent to an internment camp in the Utah desert. You might add that the author, Yoshiko Uchida, like the Sakanes, was sent to the Topaz camp in Utah.

3. Next, have students read *Journey to Topaz*. As they read, have students consider and note what everyday life at Topaz was like for the Sakane family. Specifically, have them record any special events that take place. Suggest that students use the library to find more first-person accounts of Japanese internment during World War II. You might recommend the following books as appropriate sources of information: *The Children of Topaz* by Michael O. Tunnell and George W. Chilcoat; *Farewell to Manzanar* by Jeanne Wakatsuki Houston; and *Nisei Daughter* by Monica Sone. In addition, direct students to use library resources to find pictures of the Lincoln Memorial, the Vietnam Veterans Memorial, and memorials in their town or city that commemorate famous people or events.

4. When students have completed their reading and research, organize them into small groups. Direct groups to design a memorial to be erected at the Topaz camp that will honor the Japanese Americans who were detained there. Suggest that they first study the pictures of other memorials they found during their research, and recommend that groups create similar designs for their memorials. Mention to students that memorials might include scenes of everyday life at the camp or might have elements that represent ideas—for example, the flowing water in a fountain might represent freedom. Tell students that their memorial designs should include sketches or models of the memorial and a written description that explains the symbols used. Remind students that memorial ideas should be based on the notes they made during class discussions and their reading of *Journey to Topaz,* and on the research they conducted.

5. Call on groups to present their memorial designs to the class. Conclude by asking students to discuss whether internment of American citizens, even during wartime, is justified.

ASSESSMENT

1. To assess students' memorial designs, use Rubric 3: Artwork in the *Alternative Assessment Handbook* or in a customizable format on the One-Stop Planner.

2. Additional grades can be based on students' participation in the concluding discussion.